reggae

the story of jamaican music

Published to accompany the television series
Reggae: The Story of Jamaican Music, first broadcast in 2002

Series Producer and Director   Mike Connolly
Executive Producer   Mark Cooper
Associate Producer   Lloyd Bradley
Assistant Producer   Maxine Gordon
Production Coordinator   Georgina Akibo-Betts
Production Manager   Jo Housden

First published 2002
© Lloyd Bradley 2002
The moral right of the author has been asserted

ISBN: 0 563 48807 7

Published by BBC Worldwide Ltd,
Woodlands, 80 Wood Lane, London W12 0TT

Commissioning Editor: Emma Shackleton
Production Controller: Susan Currie
Copy-editor: David Hutcheon
Editorial, design and picture research at The Foundry:
Julia Rolf, Nick Wells and Polly Willis

Colour originations by Radstock Reproductions Ltd, Midsomer Norton
Printed and bound in Great Britain by Butler & Tanner Ltd, Frome & London

reggae

the story of jamaican music

Lloyd Bradley

with photographs by
Dennis Morris

BBC

contents

The Melodians's Brent Dowe

the story of jamaican music

A friend of mine taught in Zimbabwe for a couple years, and came back saying it took him ages to get used to the local sound systems playing dub reggae all night, every night. A guy I went to school with went to Australia and Southeast Asia on business, and every time his Jamaican parentage came up in conversation, whoever he was talking to would start singing a Bob Marley song. Tokyo has a vibrant ska scene. As has Los Angeles. A Jamaican producer I know is experimenting with dancehall reggae with Portuguese vocals to meet the demand in Brazil, because the Spanish versions he's been knocking out for years do so well in the rest of South America. There's not just one veteran reggae act that spends each summer touring Europe so they can afford to do, frankly, not very much for the rest of every year. And we haven't started talking about the United Kingdom yet.

Given that Jamaica is an otherwise relatively insignificant island in the Caribbean, with a population half the size of London's and just about every post-colonial problem on the dial, that its music should have such an impact on the rest of the planet is remarkable. Then, when you take into account that a mere 45 years ago, Jamaican popular music, or any modern indigenous cultural expression, simply did not exist, reggae's story is little short of astonishing.

Street dancers in downtown Kingston

Burning Spear

Or at least it is to those underprivileged souls who have never listened to too many reggae records or spent any time at all in Jamaica. For the rest of us, how reggae's story assumed the magnitude it has is a question so elementary it rarely gets asked. And tends to get answered even less than that. What has made the difference is spirit. A spirit that has led a people out of slavery, through colonialism and is currently surviving some of the grimmest conditions – literal and economic – of anywhere in the world.

The Jamaican spirit is evident as soon as you hit the tarmac at Norman Manley Airport and start talking to Jamaicans – although after a nine-hour flight it can get mistaken for contrariness or even stroppiness. Which is kind of understandable, as, while this indomitable spirit gave birth to ska, it's the same thing that changed the beat to rock steady and then to reggae before any of these forms had, in Western terms, come to the end of their natural lives. Bizarrely, the very attitude that carried reggae to make such an impression all over the world is the self same approach that resolutely tried to keep the music for its parochial audience, determined to stay one step ahead as the rest of the world sought to share Jamaica's musical riches. Almost as if by going 'a foreign' the music somehow diluted its essential Jamaicanness and therefore needed to re-invent itself at its root in order to stay true to its original purpose.

A theory made solid by the advent of dancehall reggae. Immediately after its most successful period ever, when the likes of Burning Spear, Bob Marley and Jimmy Cliff really did conquer the world, reggae's creativity withdrew to downtown Kingston and emerged in a form that roots reggae's wider, somewhat hippified audience couldn't begin to come to grips with. Then when they did they were more than likely offended, yet it still went on to make its mark elsewhere as dancehall deejays have become a 'must have' accessory for so many of America's rock acts.

But while the singers of songs and the players of instruments have done their bit, trying to describe this spirit in conventional terms was never going to be easy. About as straightforward as explaining what smoke is to someone who's been blind all their life. However, through Dennis Morris's pictures and the interviews with and comments from a host of reggae's legends and luminaries, this book manages to come closer than it might. Many of the interviews are the result of the BBC series producer Mike Connolly's skill, insight and knowledge, while most would not have happened were it not for the patience and tenacity of Maxine Gordon and Georgina Akibo-Betts.

Dennis's skill as a photographer, in particular, has allowed him to strip away any barriers between himself and his subjects to capture people as they really are and life as it is really lived. It's in the remarkable candidness and intimacy Dennis achieves that the true spirit of Jamaica shines through for everybody to see and hopefully share in, because once you do, you'll realise there's no more appropriate way to tell the story of Jamaican music.

Lloyd Bradley, London, May 2002

1
why ska?

Rico Rodriguez

Ska was inevitable. It was always going to happen sooner rather than later. There was an explosion of music that engulfed first Kingston and then the entire island. It was as if people had been waiting for something like ska to happen. Which, in a way, they had.

As the British colonial government was winding down its business in Jamaica at the end of the 1950s, American cultural colonisation was gaining a foothold. The BBC-style Jamaican radio stations that turned out a steady flow of light classics, light jazz and light chat were being increasingly disregarded by the masses, as it became easy to pick up the powerful radio stations in the southern United States with their steady output of R&B, blues and jump jazz. These raucous, roadhouse-ish rhythms were swiftly adopted by the sound systems and showbands, but while they may have been just right for the nightclubs and dancehalls, they didn't really suit the island's overall mood. With independence looming the notion of being Jamaican took on a very different meaning, and one of the most obvious, instantly uplifting ways of expressing this notion of nationalism was with a modern Jamaican music form.

What came storming out of West Kingston to dominate the Jamaican music business between 1962 and 1964 was a galloping, uptempo,

intricately arranged and expertly played hybrid of those American forms, inasmuch as it was based on R&B and played in a big-band, jazz style, with the added Jamaicanism of switching the emphasis from the upbeat to the downbeat. Out of this exuberant music came tunes like 'Guns Of Navarone', 'Al Capone' and 'My Boy Lollipop'. But why it happened is every bit as interesting as what happened.

This being Jamaica, where popular history is oral history, there are about half a dozen different 'definitive' accounts of who actually invented ska, with as many separate takes on where, when and how. It would be virtually impossible to pin down. In the Kingston musical community people lived on top of each other, almost literally, so there wasn't much that could be kept secret or exclusive. Ideas leaked all over the place and everybody played on practically every producer's sessions. But what everybody seems to agree on is *why* it happened. Ska came about because Clement 'Coxsone' Dodd and Cecil 'Prince Buster' Campbell, two of Jamaica's most important sound system owners/record producers, had read the mood and heard the talk and wanted to change the beat. And each, independently of the other, held recording sessions that altered the standard R&B boogie rhythm into something identifiably ska. Identifiably Jamaican.

Since ska wasn't too radical a departure from its American counterpart it was easy for the sound system crowds to love it. It was uptempo and joyously celebratory; could incorporate such local flavour as Rasta drumming or snatches of mento, the Jamaican equivalent of calypso; its export was putting Jamaica on the world culture map; and as a music to dance to, it was close enough to R&B to be familiar. But ska came to dominate Jamaican culture, and this was down to the musicians involved and how they took to it.

To look at ska purely from its R&B roots is perfectly valid, as this way tells its tale through the recording of the music and the sound systems that became its best-known outlet. After all, the original Jamaican R&B/ska recordings were made before there was any record industry worth speaking about on the island. Discs were cut almost solely for sound systems, and any obvious developments were dictated by the soundmen; like the 'invention' of ska itself. This meant there was an air of formality, as each single was about two-and-a-half minutes with a certain structure that drew on R&B. But while this route provides a handy set of milestones to plot the music's evolution, it doesn't get to the driving force behind it. In fact ska came of age as the exciting, organically mutating music that continues to thrill crowds in clubs and on the bandstands, and in this it owes more to jazz than to R&B.

In the early 1960s, Kingston nightlife involved about as much live music as it did sound systems. The big lawns featured bands for a lot of the time and the tonier clubs wouldn't have anything else – establishments such as the Glass Bucket and the Silver Slipper boasted about their orchestras. The onset of ska had injected a new vigour into an already vibrant scene, as it replaced Latin and American sounds and began to attract a younger, livelier crowd. As it developed it offered, too, opportunities that were as much about creativity as potential earning.

The backbone of the Jamaican music industry had always been its jazz players, guys that were formally trained at establishments like the Alpha Boys' School or the Stony Hill Military School, and served apprenticeships playing light jazz or danceable Top 40 covers for American tourists in the north coast hotels. If you were serious about your music you went 'a foreign', to New York or London, where you could play some proper jazz. The likes of Joe Harriott, Dizzy Reece and Monty Alexander carved enormous reputations away from Jamaica – indeed, there were enough professional musicians on the SS *Empire Windrush*'s famous voyage bringing the first wave of Jamaican immigrants to the UK to put together a very creditable below-decks dance band. The arrival of ska, however, created a situation in which musical giants such as Don Drummond, Tommy McCook, Roland Alphonso, Lester Sterling and John 'Dizzy' Moore could show off and grow their skills without having to leave home.

In the dancehall, this new music created its own jazz-style situation. The rigid structures that allowed ska (barely) to contain itself on record provided the perfect framework on stage for the front men to get to work. No longer confined to copying American swing bands from the stock arrangements that could be bought at any music store, Jamaican players responded with gusto.

The classic ska line-up was between 10 and 20 players, sitting on the bandstand. They were rhythm-driven and horn-heavy, with the soloists working to impress each other as much as the paying customers. Each was determined to outdo his fellows with musical audacity as much as conventional skills. A rhythm section as completely reliable as The Skatalites' Lloyd Knibbs (drums) and Lloyd Brevett (bass) would guarantee the soloists the space and the support to go wherever their abilities took them. And with guys as gifted as trombonist Don Drummond, saxman Tommy McCook and guitarist Ernest Ranglin, there appeared to be no outer limit. Cutting contests were par for the course at any of the livelier establishments, often becoming so intense that they took over from the action on the dance-floor. PJ Patterson, the Jamaican Prime Minister at the time of writing, gets misty-eyed when he tells of a monumental musical battle between Drummond and Ranglin that did all but stop traffic in the street outside and was talked about for weeks afterwards.

It was the excitement and adventure presented by ska that established the Jamaican music industry. Creditable musicians stayed at home where they had an art form they could feel proud to be a part of and call their own. With players of such calibre to work with, the producers could keep things moving on in the studio and so plot a path of development for the island's first indigenous modern music.

Derrick Morgan

By 1964 ska was starting to wind down in favour of the much more mannered and blatantly American influenced rock steady. This new music was very different: far more vocal-oriented and American soul-based as it drew inspiration and harmony patterns from groups such as The Impressions and The Drifters. It also required smaller bands with an increasing reliance on electric instrumentation. Significantly, rock steady was far more a studio music than ska, therefore it was developed by record producers rather than on the bandstand. This became something of a pattern for the Jamaican music business that remains in place today, where recording is held in much higher regard than live performance. As a result, the golden age of ska was the last time jazz influenced the island's industry to any degree and soon the players being turned out by places such as Alpha were once again having to look abroad.

Ernest Ranglin

'My Boy Lollipop': The Inside Story

In 1964, ska took on a properly international profile with 'My Boy Lollipop' – recorded in the UK by the Jamaican singer Millie Small and released on a Dutch record label. Selling more than seven million copies, the tune was a hit in the US, Africa and the UK, where it reached Number Two. The song was a cover of an old US R&B hit by Barbie Gaye, and guitarist Ernest Ranglin was the man who arranged the song in a ska style suitable for the mainstream market. He remembers how it happened:

'I was the first A&R man for Island Records, and Chris Blackwell had asked me to go to England because ska was taking off a bit there – this was 1963. The tunes were just piano, bass, guitar, drums, and there were no proper arrangements. Chris said I'd do very well if I came to England and put some arrangements to the tunes people were starting to do. So I went.

'This was in October, about two weeks after I arrived, and we had a very good Sunday, nice and sunny, so Chris decided to go to Brighton. It was Chris, myself and Millie Small, a young singer who had come over to England with Chris before I arrived. On the way down, Chris started talking about wanting to find a tune for her because he believed that if she could find the right tune to get her started she would last about ten years. Millie liked the song "My Boy Lollipop", and on the way down she started singing it. Chris seemed to go along with it, and as she started singing it with a natural Jamaican style it began to sound much more like a ska song and I started to hum a background, what I would do with the tune.

'I was thinking about it all day, so by the time we got back to London I've got it pretty much worked out. On Monday, we were at the Lansdowne Studios and I've gone in straight and arranged the tune.

'People say it's not a real ska tune, but it is, it's just not ska like we did with Theophilus Beckford which is much slower, almost like rock steady. We knew it had to be faster because when we came to England we used to go to these teenage parties at the weekend and take records. They would play them and we would watch the reaction of the people and they much preferred the fast ones. Maybe because of weather conditions, but they needed it faster to get anything going. So we made Millie's ska much faster – if you notice, a lot of the blue beat ska is faster, because that's what gets the English blood going.'

Ska in America

By 1964, ska had moved uptown and *all* Jamaicans acknowledged it as *their* music. As a result, the government realised they had a) something to sell; and b) something that would help sell the island in their push to attract the new 'jet setting' tourists. They attempted to sell ska to the rest of the world in much the same way as you'd sell auto parts by taking it to the World's Fair in New York. A kind of funky trade delegation.

Former record producer and future Prime Minister Edward Seaga, a committed supporter of indigenous Jamaican culture, was, as Head of Social

Millie Small

Welfare and Economic Development, the minister responsible for the event. Byron Lee ran an established show band who had mastered ska. Lee remembers the mission as a valiant try:

'Mr Seaga had some record company people come down from New York to advise us on how we could break this music internationally. We talked about the dance, the ska, because every other style of music that became popular back then had a dance that went with it – the twist, the jerk, the hully gully … all dances. So we had to choreograph the ska dance and use that to break the music itself in the Jamaican pavilion at the World's Fair.

'My group, Byron Lee & The Dragonaires, went as the backing band and the singers that were going to perform were The Blues Busters, Prince Buster, Jimmy Cliff and Monty Morris and six dancers, four women and two men. The dancers would start off and get everybody in the audience to stand up and do the ska. That way they got adjusted to the beats before the singers came out and the audience had to adjust to the melodies.

'We worked hard, and they were good shows, but the ska didn't catch on from them. It didn't have the support that it had in England, where the Jamaicans know that it's something coming from their yard and they'll give it enough support and make noise to get it started. You didn't have that migration of Jamaicans to America yet, so there was no concentration of Jamaicans like in London. And in those days Jamaicans didn't have their own radio stations or even their own programmes.

'It was Millie Small went big with the ska in America with "My Boy Lollipop", but she came in from London.'

Edward Seaga, however, is rather more forthright as to why it wasn't an unqualified success:

'We took it to the wrong country. The United States wasn't ready for it. Ska was becoming popular in Britain. I said let's try the US. The World's Fair was going on at the time and we sent a team of artists to see if it would stir any interest.

'Well, it didn't. We were before our time and the United States wasn't ready for that kind of music. At that time, the United States didn't react well to rhythmic music, the popular music was still standard and traditional. And, at the same time, African-Americans were not a very strong segment of the population insofar as record purchases were concerned.

'I would have liked it to have done well there, but as it turned out, it was probably good that we didn't because it was too early in its development to have moved that fast. It could have stopped it developing as a genuine Jamaican music.'

Although the American public didn't exactly take to ska, the US music business was slightly more adventurous and was determined to give it a go. Atlantic Records put out *Jamaican Ska* and *Jamaica Jump Up*, two ska albums by Byron Lee & The Dragonaires, who for that moment had renamed themselves The Ska Kings; Epic Records went, rather pointedly, with *The REAL Jamaican Ska*, a compilation of Jamaican tunes; and, at the other end of the credibility spectrum, ABC-Paramount recorded a ska album by the white American R&B singer Steve Alaimo.

Lloyd Brevett on Ska

Lloyd Brevett was the original Skatalites' bass player. Together with drummer Lloyd Knibbs, he was responsible for the locked-down rhythm section that held so much ska in place. With these two behind them, soloists like Don Drummond, Tommy McCook or Roland Alphonso could take off and fly, secure in the knowledge that when they came back down to earth the beat would be exactly where they left it.

'A set of musicians get together in Jamaica and start playing. We play in bands in the clubs and hotels, where we play stock arrangements – arrangements of well-known songs that the band leader would buy, usually from America, printed on sheet music – or we play jazz. We go on like that for a while, but then say we want to make some music for ourselves, *our own music*. So out of that same jazz we change the style of the rhythm by having the guitar play that *chank! chank! chank*! and the drummer play the down beat instead of the up beat he'd play in jazz.'

'From that day it was important and still is to this day. It was our type of music that could lift up the youth and make Jamaica known around the world. The people loved it, they follow us anywhere. At independence, they made a float, a big tall truck with flowers, with The Skatalites on top of it and we played right through the city of Kingston, with people running and walking behind it. The whole city.'

'We were the musicians who would be called in by producers to play ska to back singers. We were the first band that is really doing it and staying together – we stayed together for two or three years – so people hear that music and start asking for us to play for them. It was me, on bass, Lloyd [Knibbs] the drummer, Tommy McCook on sax, he was really the leader, Roland Alphonso on sax, Don Drummond on trombone, Jah Jerry on guitar, Dizzy Moore on trumpet, Jackie Mittoo was the keyboard player.

'They were all very good musicians. Many of them were the youths that were at the Alpha Boys' School or Stony Hill School where they all had very good musical training. They could all read music and write music. They had been properly trained by army musicians. I didn't go to Alpha, my dad was a very good bass player and he taught me the bass. Then everybody had played in Jamaican bands like Eric Dean's orchestra or Roy Coburn's big bands, where they had to be able to play not just calypso, but rhumba and jazz as well. The Skatalites was the best set of musicians ever to come out of Jamaica.'

Lloyd Brevett

The Alpha Boys' School

In terms of the development of Jamaican music nothing can compare with the Alpha Boys' School. The cream of Jamaican brass players such as Don Drummond, Rico Rodriguez, Tommy McCook, Eddie 'Tan Tan' Thornton, John 'Dizzy' Moore, Joe Harriott, Cedric Brooks, Lester Sterling, Dizzy Reece, Harold McNair, Wilton Gaynair, Vin Gordon and Bobby Ellis were all members of the school's marching band. Indeed it's a pretty safe bet that without Alpha there would have been no ska.

Alpha School was founded on its South Camp Road site in 1880 by the Catholic order The Sisters Of Mercy as a residential school for wayward boys and has always put an emphasis on strict discipline. The boys wear uniforms, but no shoes or socks, perform chores, wait in orderly lines for just about everything and learn a sense of communal and individual responsibility through what is expected of them. But it has a purpose, as Sister Ignatius, who has been at Alpha since 1939, explains:

'The Alpha Boys' School is a school that caters for the unfortunate. It teaches them trades so they can earn a living when they leave. The boys we get are the boys that are either in trouble or going to get into trouble. Boys that don't go to school or their parents can't manage them. Their parents might put them in here or they go to Family Court, where they might be sent here or to any other children's home. We try to put them right and send them out when they are sixteen as useful people.'

Sister Ignatius is in charge of music at Alpha, and their band is her particular pride and joy. It presented something of an easy option for Alpha boys as it was taken so seriously by the school that being good enough to get in the band meant you could skip certain chores – usually kitchen detail – to go to band practice.

'The band started in 1892, as a fife and drum band. That wasn't by design, as back then a Sister from England, Sister DeShantelle-Higgins, asked a gentleman in England to send some instruments to the school and he sent down drums and fifes, so that is what we had and we formed the marching band. Then in 1908, the school received a donation of brass instruments from America for us, so we carried on with a marching band, but with brass instruments.'

The formality of the musical teaching at Alpha gives their graduates a solid grounding. The boys learn to read and write music, are taught music theory, have to know their instruments inside out and must master the classics before they're encouraged to start improvising. The idea is that they become so proficient at the basics and foundation skills that they can go anywhere and play in any style.

Which seemed to work, as it wasn't unusual for nightclub band leaders to be sending Ernest Ranglin down to Alpha to sweet talk Sister Ignatius into letting her youthful charges play in clubs they weren't old enough to officially get into. It was believed that Alpha boys were good enough to immediately fit in even if they'd never seen the arrangements before. It was a backbone of Alpha horn players that made The Skatalites, Jamaica's best ever original backing band, and to hear today's young school band run through a selection of Skatalites hits, it's obvious Alpha traditions are still very much alive.

Above: Queuing for lunch at the school. How many
future greats are in this line?

Right: Sister Ignatius in the Alpha Boys meeting room

Don Drummond

One of the greatest musicians Jamaica has ever produced was trombonist Don Drummond. A deeply introverted and apparently complex character, his work was almost exclusively domestic – he never went abroad to pursue his jazz dream like Ernest Ranglin, Joe Harriott or Monty Alexander – although he was universally acknowledged as being one of the all-time greats.

Don Drummond began his love affair with the trombone at the Alpha Boys' School, where he stood out as a scholar to such a degree he would be in demand by the nightclub orchestras of the day when he was barely out of short trousers. Playing big-band jazz at places like the Glass Bucket and the Silver Slipper, Drummond's soloing could literally bring the dance floor to a standstill, especially if he was involved in a cutting contest with a colleague or a young challenger from outside. He moved on to ska as one of the brightest stars in The Skatalites, recording for Duke Reid and Coxsone Dodd and bringing his jazz chops to proceedings when he arrived at rehearsals with fabulous solos and melody lines written out so that the others could fall into place behind him.

Although he learned his craft in the calm, ordered world of a marching band and ska is usually remembered as being on the breathless side of frantic, Drummond's style was particularly fluid, and he could bring a hazy, far more mellifluous feel to proceedings. In his hands, the trombone, never the most cheerful of instruments, took on a melancholy air that would appear to reflect his troubled state of mind. He wrote largely in minor keys and, as an early convert to Rastafari, he would write tunes with a wailing, journey-to-Addis feel half a decade before roots reggae made that sort of behaviour fashionable. 'Eastern Standard Time', 'Addis Ababa', 'Alipang' and 'Cool Smoke' are four tracks that showcase Don Drummond at his most affecting and mournful dread.

It's said at the more, er, respectable end of Kingston's musical community veterans that it was Drummond's excessive ganja consumption that lead to his final tragedy. On New Year's Eve 1965 he failed to turn up for a band engagement and at some time the next day turned himself in at a police station having stabbed to death his common-law wife, the nightclub dancer Marguerita. There was no doubt of his guilt, but, according to his defence lawyer, future Prime Minister PJ Patterson:

'At the trial, he was in no position to give us any verbal instructions, but there was no doubt she had died by his hand. We went purely on the basis of his medical condition and the jury retired for less than an hour before they returned a unanimous verdict of not guilty by virtue of insanity.'

It was most likely due to undiagnosed schizophrenia rather than excessive weed, as Drummond had been checking himself into Bellevue mental hospital for increasing lengths of time for several years before this. It was there he died in 1969. His funeral – of traffic-stopping proportions – was paid for by his fellow musicians.

Lloyd Brevett said of him: 'He was not a man who wrote whole tunes, the bass line and all that, he just wrote his part. But he don't make no trouble, he was a quiet brother.'

Don Drummond

2
the people's radio

Sound systems are great, cumbersome, need-a-furniture-van-to-transport-them, loud, usually home-made, apparently frighteningly unsophisticated affairs. For decades, there was no point in making a record in Jamaica if it wasn't going to get played at a sound system dance.

It is impossible to underestimate the sound systems' significance in the development, attitude and sustainment of the music from ska to dancehall and all points in between. While it's probably a bit of literary licence to say that without these (originally) uniquely Jamaican situations the music is unlikely to have progressed at all, it wouldn't have moved nearly as fast or as interestingly. It was the sound system operators' competitiveness that pushed them to come up with new music and new dances to go with it.

Then there's the matter of keeping it 'real', so to speak, the very important aspect of keeping Jamaican music on track, whereby it remains true to itself and its immediate audience – Jamaican sound system crowds. The only way the stylistic myriad of twists and turns stays essentially organic instead of force-fed with somebody else's require-ments is through the sound systems. In fact, as soon as reggae, in whatever form, moves away from its sound system roots and starts playing by

other rules, it goes off the rails pretty quick. Witness Shabba Ranks's American adventures. It's therefore no coincidence that, with only a few notable exceptions, the best Jamaican record producers have either been soundmen or had close links with a sound system.

Pure and simple, sound systems are what make Jamaican music so special and so unique; they are the reason an island with a population half the size of London's can produce music of the quantity and quality it has for the past 40-odd years. Because Jamaican music has this singular bond with its audience – for both live and recorded performances – it has maintained this phenomenal level of creativity, and it's at the sound system dances where the relationship is consummated.

The sound system's significance in modern Jamaican music goes back to a time before there was any modern Jamaican music. Back to those pre-ska, pre-independence days of the 1950s, when R&B was carrying the swing. At that time, sound system lawns were among the main sources of entertainment in Kingston's inner city and, given that there were few radios and even fewer record players, one of the only opportunities for many people to hear recorded music. The idea of building a decent rig and playing records for the public – instead of the far more financially prohibitive hiring of a band – opened dancehall promotions up to a greater number of operators, and, thus, music in general to a much larger potential audience.

Alongside the steady diet of imported R&B, the early sound system operators like Tom 'The Great' Sebastian and Count Smith 'The Blues Blaster' would spin a degree of jazz and country, plus a sprinkling of latin, particularly Colombian merengue and Cuban mambo, to provide a rocking, but inexpensive alternative to the big-band nightclub sessions. Remarkably, it's still possible to step back into those early sound system days at Kingston's legendary Ray Town Sunday night dances, where they have seriously old-time sessions where it wouldn't be unusual to hear tunes by Tammy Wynette, Pérez Prado and Louis Prima alongside Louis Jordan and Johnny Ventura, with 'couple dancing' making something of a comeback.

It was at the second generation of sound system lawn dances (so named for obvious, *al fresco* reasons) that Jamaican music itself was born, as a younger, more ambitious and more competitive generation of operators took up the reins. In order to keep ahead of their opposition, keen guys like Coxsone Dodd and Prince Buster began sponsoring their own recording sessions.

Initially, the recordings would be R&B or its island counterpart, Jamaican boogie, but then the soundmen were pushed towards ska by a combination of striving to have something different to play at their dances and, as independence fever swept the country, the desire to create something intrinsically Jamaican. Quite apart from creating a new music that was both endearing and enduring, there were two circumstances that shaped the Jamaican music business in a form that still holds true. By happening downtown in the ordinary people's dancehalls, the creation of Jamaica's first pop music became theirs and such ownership is still assumed. Secondly, it established the idea of soundmen as record producers, a trend that exists in Jamaican music to this day, continuing to keep the sound system at the heart of the recording process.

Thus the Jamaican music business and the Jamaican people forged their alliance. The soundman who was relying on crowds for gate money or liquor sales worked to keep his crowds large and happy, and this same audience, who quite rightly believed this was *their* music, felt they had the right to more than just voting with their feet and would instantly, loudly and not always good-naturedly criticise anything they were less than happy about. Such instant interactivity meant the soundman always had to pay close attention to his crowds, and so recordings were always more than merely influenced by the popular mood – they were pretty well dictated by it. Still are, pretty much. Then, in the early 1960s, as the soundmen began making recordings for sale, as opposed to

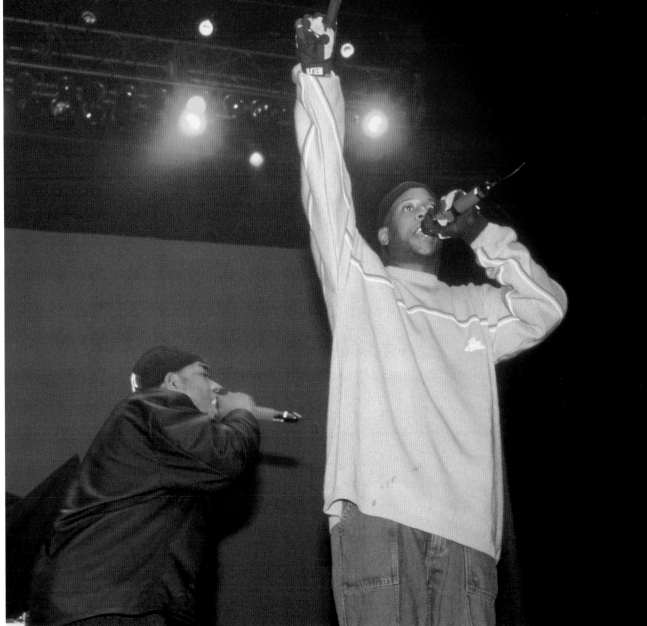

Black Star

just making them for sound system use, it was even more crucial to road test what they were doing in the dancehall, and so keep the audience closely involved with what trends were being set. And the people concerned took their responsibilities seriously – the importance of sound system loyalty grew as it became a territorial thing and crowds wanted to do their bit for their man by supporting new songs and popularising new dances or by saving him from himself by rejecting anything ill-conceived. To give an idea of the level of affinity, soundmen would frequently repay their public's loyalty to a tune that had made a big impact by keeping it unique to his sound system for months before he'd release it, allowing his crowd to feel special about 'their' tune. The fact that this served to hype a tune before he put it into the shops was immaterial.

As time went on and the Jamaican music industry expanded, the sound systems provided a vital promotional service for all producers, whether they had a sound system or not. Because until very recently, Jamaican radio played very little reggae and what it did play was seldom the kind of cutting-edge stuff that the little grass-roots studios were putting out, the sound systems were the only places the number of records being made could reach their potential audience. There was also a lot of talk about the prohibitive cost of greasing the right palms to get a record on the radio, and while you'd still probably have to shell out to get your tune on a particular sound system, at least you were keeping the money in the community. This is when producers who didn't own sound systems were completely tuned into the notion that the record business (as opposed to a music business) needed a link with a sound system. Bunny Lee is a shining example – he didn't own a sound system but maintained very close ties with King Tubby's and became one of rock steady and reggae's most consistently successful record producers.

Perhaps most important though, as time marched on, was that sound systems provided a refuge for reggae when it wanted to regenerate after straying too far from its roots. We'll look at this in greater detail later, but throughout its short life, Jamaican popular music has run in a series of cycles that have seen each particular style do very well in the outside world, and, as if that success somehow divorces itself from its home crowd in Kingston's dancehalls, it reinvents itself. Often it would be exclusively designed to please the home crowd and always via the sound systems, as that's where it interacts with the people. Rock steady, reggae, roots, dancehall, ragga, slackness and so on, you'd hear them first on the sound systems.

Nowadays, though, the importance of the sound system seems to be waning. There's much more reggae radio and one Jamaican TV station seems to show nothing but booty call dancehall videos. Then there's the chance to break America, giving producers many more options. In early 2002, two or three big dancehall producers told me that instead of cutting dub plates of new tunes to give to the sound systems, they're burning CDs to send to the radio stations. And King Jammy's, one of the biggest sounds in Kingston, rarely gets taken out of its trailer these days.

True, this represents modernisation within the reggae industry, but you can't help thinking that when it does move away from its roots it starts to wither. Worryingly, if it starts behaving like just another pop music style, it won't be long before it starts to sound like one.

King Jammy's

King Jammy's on Jamaica's Sound System Traditions

'My sound system, King Jammy's Super Power went all over the island and played in every parish, it was big. Whenever a producer have a new song or I voice a song in the studio, we would cut it in the dub room on an acetate and send it out on the sound system. We'd get instant feedback from the guys who operate the sound because they'd be monitoring the crowd's reaction to it. Sometimes I'd go myself and we'd know exactly what the people there think of that particular tune, so we'd know when to release it.

'All the sound systems worked like that, which is a tradition in Jamaican music because in those earlier days we couldn't get no radio play. They used to play pure foreign songs on the radio, or just the very big established Jamaican producers.

I never used to get no play, nor did anyone else just coming into the music. So the sound systems were vital to anybody who didn't have the clout to get their songs on the radio, as it was the only way people could get to hear them. They were the lifeblood of the reggae business.

'They're not as important as they once were though, because there's more radio stations and the radio plays so much reggae that producers don't need to rely on the sound systems so much. When we do a new song these days instead of cut a dub for the sound system, we burn it on a CD and send it out to the radio stations and get feedback that way. In many ways, it's better for us because the radio covers the whole island all the time and more people listen to the radio than go to sound system dances.

'There's only about four or five big sound systems in Jamaica now and they play in smaller clubs a lot rather than lawn dances – Stone Love, Metro Media, Renaissance and a couple of others. My sound system has sort of retired, it just come out for oldies dances these days, because it's so difficult. Sound systems need a special permit these days; and they've come down on sound men with a charge of making excessive noise in public. People that live in the hills around Kingston that don't appreciate loud music are always calling the police. They would fine you and if you did it twice they either charge you a larger sum or seize your sound system for a while. They were always seizing sound systems and it got too much for many soundmen so they just packed up.'

The Mighty Two: Duke Reid and Coxsone Dodd

Arthur 'Duke' Reid and Coxsone Dodd were original sound system competitors, each trying to outdo each other, pulling the biggest crowds or selling the most beer or breaking their own new tunes; it was a matter of honour. Brent Dowe was there:

'Duke Reid and Sir Coxsone were the number one and number two sound systems on the island at the time. When they were playing records they were playing against each other, so when they were making records it was against each other – like a competition, all the time. If you were singing for one, you couldn't go and sing for the other, or if you did you couldn't go back to the first one for a long time. They were like that.

'The sound system was the order of the day back then, it was a goldmine. This is where people come every week, every day … anywhere they play is a crowd, and they have the new tunes to play so it was a serious business.

'The whole of this area, Bond Street, was Duke Reid followers, they used to say Duke Reid's sound is better than Coxsone's, while Coxsone had his own crowd in his own area. These people used to travel and follow the Duke Reid sound. Anywhere he play, all these people would leave Bond Street and Charles Street just to go where he is at. He had his protection too, "chucker outs", who would damage you if you say anything about Duke Reid or try to damage his sound. They were his men and used to protect him so you couldn't touch his sound. Coxsone had his own protectors too,

because each of these sound systems had followers and most of the time they are at war with each other. Real war, fights. Man get chop up, get hurt, just to say Duke Reid's sound is better than Coxsone. A Coxsone man might stab you or a Duke Reid man might stab you if you say the wrong thing. It was a very serious rivalry.

'They didn't actually fight, although their supporters would try and do things, Coxsone and Duke Reid themselves didn't organise anything. They was always trying to get the better crowds and they clash a couple of times – play music against each other, but they never fight.

'In the last days, before Duke died, I'm told they became very close, they became good friends and would phone one another and talk. They could see what each was doing so they join forces.'

Duke Reid

Coxsone Dodd outside his American record store

The Greatest of Them All: King Tubby's Home Town HiFi

Dennis Alcapone used to deejay a sound system called El Paso, but the sound system he looks back at with understandably misty eyes is King Tubby's Home Town HiFi, the technologically marvellous rig owned and operated by the great King Tubby's.

'Dances used to be nice, you'd have some violence, of course, but on a very low level, mostly domestic squabbles and arguments. Those was the days of the big sound systems, you had the eighteen-inch speakers and they'd have speaker boxes with two or four of those in – massive. We used to call those speaker boxes Houses of Joy. In the 1970s they cut them down a bit and go for

quality and start calling sound systems "hifi" and they moved from a big tube [valve] in the amplifier called the 8070 down to a tube called the KT88. Those new tubes make the bass more rounder and sweet – the 8070 make the speaker box sound "woof!" and vibrate, but the KT88 cut that right down and make the bass sound round. It was King Tubby's introduced them to Jamaica.

'King Tubby's HiFi was one of the greatest sounds ever to come out of Jamaica. He was an electrical genius. He introduced reverb and echo, because it was the craze among deejays for when you are talking on the mic, but you could only have it in the studio, Tubby's actually brought it into the dancehall … "*this coming Saturday night night night, all roads lead lead lead*." It was wonderful, and the first time he did it nobody know he could do it and when the reverb come out into the night air …

'His sound could be heard all over the area, because he'd get one of his workers to climb trees and put the steel horns way in top of the trees, so the high frequencies would carry the sound right over Kingston. Then, with the speakers underneath the trees playing the mid-range and bass the sound was magnificent. In the night, when the breeze is blowing and the music playing, it was like a heavenly sound. Beautiful.

'Tubby's was that big in Jamaica you would have most other producers carry their pre-release tunes for Tubby's to play to promote their music, or they'd just want to hear what it sound like on a sound system that good.

'The people loved it. They really loved it, so much he couldn't keep no more dance than what he was doing. The dance so sweet as well, why would anybody start fighting when the music's so nice? You would see the beer truck pull up at the dance, load off beer before the dancehall and then the following day they're taking pure empty box. Everything sell off! That's how much people used to enjoy themselves. Man used to hold woman and rub with them … it was so nice.'

Sound Systems in the UK

In the 1970s, before Soul II Soul were making records or even hosting their legendary Africa Centre warehouse parties, they were a traditional reggae sound system called Jah Rico, operating in North London in exactly the way British sound systems have done since the 1950s. It was their understanding of how sound system culture worked in the UK, how they as second and third generation Caribbean immigrants wanted something different out of the experience and what the mainstream would want from a sound system, that enabled them to become Soul II Soul.

What it also did, was introduce the British mainstream to sound system culture in a way that was fairly unadulterated but at the same time not scary at all. More than merely thumping bass, darkened rooms and seamless music, they created the sense of community and identity that had been at the foundation of the British sound system scene. In the UK sound system dances, or blues dances as they were called, were vital gathering places for black people who felt excluded from the regular British social life and wanted to create a piece of home for themselves where they could relax among their own. It was a vital escape hatch.

This was before rave culture, a scene that has strong parallels with the long-established sound system world, established itself in the UK. Soul II Soul's success is one more example of how reggae and reggae's way of doing things have greatly influenced mainstream British youth culture.

Soul II Soul in action

3
sweet harmonies

Delroy Wilson

Talk to practically anybody in Jamaica and they'll tell you about Jamaicans' special relationship with music. It's what put Jamaica on the world map: the most famous Jamaican in history is a musician; the Song Of The Millennium, 'One Love', was Jamaican; and it is the country's most lucrative legal export.

Where this unique relationship manifests itself is in singing. It's more than just the singers everybody knows about too. For every Jimmy Cliff or Bob Marley or John Holt or Gregory Isaacs or Garnett Silk, there'll be a hundred impromptu performances every hour at bus stops, in workshops, on streets, in vegetable patches, in cars … anywhere. Jamaicans approach singing like other nations breathe in and out or put on underwear in the morning – it's a natural part of the way of their world. Jamaicans sing to express their joy at life, celebrate a particular event, ease the pressure, make a task go faster, or a walk less tedious, or just because they fancy it.

This is something, most Jamaicans will agree, that was handed down from slavery through colonialism, and it seems likely that the rebel roots of Jamaica's modern music were put down in the seventeenth century along with the people's propensity for song. The church is frequently cited as being at the back of the Jamaican love affair

with song, and if you go back a few hundred years, the acts of rebellion and of worship were pretty much inseparable.

Jamaica had proportionately far more slave revolts than any other island in the Caribbean – it was virtually in a state of constant civil war and normally some sort of punishment for the English gentry who were sent out there by their plantation-owning families – and the drum was soon banned as a means of communication and a show of spirit. Singing soon took over as a show of defiance and a celebration of African roots. When the slaves were allowed Christianity, they adapted it into something more relevant to where they were from than where they had been taken. Singing was the mainstay of services, as worshipping became an act of enormous celebration – just like it had been in Africa – and the slaves' services transferred much of their native religions' presentation methods to the New World. So much of this survives, literally, as Pocomania and Kumina, where dialects and speech

Horace Andy chilling in Jones Town, Kingston

patterns have been traced back directly to the Central Africa of centuries ago. But far more relevant, this became an approach to life that, culturally, continues to dictate the Jamaican relationship with song.

What is universally considered to be the golden age of Jamaican music – the rock-steady era – is a period when singing ruled the grooves and consummated the people's relationship with song in a way that made perfect sense in modern Jamaica. And the fact that it wasn't until the end of the ska era that singing made its mark isn't really too surprising either. It wasn't that there wasn't the will, there simply wasn't very much opportunity: the big bands that performed in the north coast hotels were mostly swing jazz or Latin, that tended not to use singers, and they didn't need them. Vocalists were (slightly) more popular in the Kingston nightclubs, but they had no lasting impact beyond that circuit because there wasn't a recording industry back then. When ska rolled around, even though it was essentially and deliberately a Jamaican music, it did not make use of the vast reserve of raw talent in the city's tenements, largely because there wasn't too much room for a singer – the real attraction of ska was in its general raucous-ness and its jazz-style showing off.

Although mighty voices such as The Maytals, Millie Small, Jimmy Cliff and Prince Buster or the line-ups of The Wailers or The Jiving Juniors did manage to make their mark, ska remained an instrumentalist's music. It's not by chance that the first ska act that comes to most people's minds is a big band, The Skatalites.

Some say one of the reasons ska was relatively quickly displaced by rock steady is because the former offered little scope for the people at large. Ska's popularity had stimulated enormous popular interest in domestic music as much more than something merely to be enjoyed at a dance. There was the nationalistic pride angle: doing something obviously Jamaican in this new independent nation; it would win you instant respect as the successful ska musicians were all heroes in and beyond their neighbourhoods; and it represented a real chance to escape from poverty and maybe to see a bit of the world. But many who were seriously into the music couldn't get into the music business because they weren't virtuoso musicians. A style that called on singers as its stars was going to change all that because you didn't need anything other than your voice and a bit of practice.

While that might be *one* reason, it was only one of several. A deliberately vocal-friendly style was on the cards because by the mid-1960s, selling records had become the end product of the music business's process, so it suited producers to shift the emphasis away from instrumentalists – especially big bands – towards singers who were far easier to manipulate and, ultimately, exploit; a situation made considerably easier for those in charge by the enormous number of singers and would-be singers queuing up outside their studios. Whatever the reasons, though, the fact remains that once rock steady did happen, there was an explosion in the number of Jamaican singers who powered the style forward.

Alton Ellis

Rock steady was what so many of Jamaica's young hopefuls had been waiting for as they practised their singing and harmonising to sound like the new American style known as soul. The rawer R&B had been supplanted by this much smoooover way of approaching a song, which found enormous favour on the island when it became popular on the airwaves, thanks to both domestic radio and the southern American stations that were getting even more powerful. American soul acts toured Jamaica regularly, and among the most popular were Curtis Mayfield's Impressions, who provided the template for so many of the rock steady trios. Most memorable is The Wailers, who, during their skinny suit period, went so far as to ape an Impressions album sleeve right down to the group's 'casual' pose.

Aping that three-part close harmony singing became something of a rock steady house style; groups like The Paragons, The Jamaicans, The Sensations, The Melodians, Justin Hinds & The Dominoes, The Three Tops, The Gaylads, Carlton & His Shoes, Slim Smith & The Uniques and The Techniques all owed a debt to The Impressions. Even in spite of independence and an apparent wave of nationalistic pride, it's a testament to the persisting power of the outside influence in Jamaican music that trios should virtually wipe out the duos that had been popular during the ska years – you'd think you'd need less instead of more lung power under these gentler circumstances. Of course there were solo artists; Bob Andy and Marcia Griffiths came good in this period, before teaming up for their pop-reggae hits of a few years later; Dobby Dobson was a rock steady star; as was Freddy McKay. Interestingly, quite a few singers who had started in the ska era seemed to have been waiting for something more suitable to come along: of them, Alton Ellis, Delroy Wilson and Roy Shirley began to show what they were really capable of.

Duke Reid, who wasn't a jazzman like Coxsone or a musical adventurer like Prince Buster, hadn't really got on with ska and relished the prospect of something silkier. Also, the idea of rock steady being an essentially American style appealed to the Duke's tastes, which were deeply conservative, and in a quaintly old-fashioned way he still believed that what came in from abroad was superior. But he produced some of the best music ever to come out of Jamaica – most of the aforementioned acts passed through his Treasure Isle studios, with several staying for the long term. When Dodd and Buster followed suit with some equally top-drawer rock steady, the singing methods became so established it carried on beyond the style itself.

As we'll see when we look at the roots period of the 1970s, some of its greatest music was classic close three-part harmonising applied to roots

The Heptones

Above: 'I think the power of music is in love songs because everyday people fall in love, Gregory Isaacs doesn't fall in love, Gregory Isaacs stands in love.'

Leroy Sibbles

material – The Mighty Diamonds, The Abyssinians, Culture and Israel Vibration were all steeped in rock steady, but their music possessed a wider subject matter than affairs of the heart. The Congos started life as a duo for their first single and when Lee Perry recorded their classic album *Heart Of The Congos*, he brought in the baritone Watty Burnett to supplement Cedric Myton and Roy Johnson to give himself three voices to work with.

There aren't too many new trios recording today, but so many of the old acts are in bigger demand than they ever were and with the likes of T.O.K. and Morgan Heritage bringing harmony

singing back, it would seem to be only a matter of time before close three-part harmonies start tearing up the dancehall again.

A Nation Sings

Under the leadership of Leroy Sibbles, The Heptones became one of Jamaica's most accomplished vocal groups ever, and as he was Studio One's musical director and in-house bass player, their rhythms were always a cut above the rest. Through a string of hits such as 'Book Of Rules', 'Party Time', 'Pretty Looks Isn't All' and 'I've Got The Handle', their three-part harmonising was a textbook example of the Jamaican approach to vocals during the latter part of the 1960s. So it is with some authority that Sibbles can explain why so many of his countrymen sing.

When did Jamaica's love for singing explode into the music business?

'It really started with rock steady, because it got a lot slower and then all kind of different singers come out. There were a lot of duos and a lot of groups. The Techniques, The Gaylads, The Wailers, The Clarendonians, The Ethiopians … even Burning Spear wasn't a solo singer then, he had two back-up singers to make a trio.'

Why was there so much three-part harmonising at that time?

'This kind of music was directly influenced by American R&B and that's where the three-part singing came from. We were very influenced by The Impressions who used to come to perform here. All the big R&B and soul acts came here - the only one that didn't was Otis Redding. It was probably The Impressions that most people tried to copy because in that era there were so many trios that sung in that style – The Melodians, The Paragons, The Jamaicans, The Sensations, Justin Hinds & The Dominoes and, of course, The Heptones.'

Why did so many young Jamaicans form vocal groups?

'Singing is part of the heritage and culture in Jamaica – from the revival churches, from the African traditional culture. Singing is in almost every family, and then in the ghetto you'll find more singers than anywhere else because it's a thing we used to do to pass the time away. It's a thing you use to soothe your spirit, your soul. And it was easy for a group to come together because you don't need a guitar, you don't need drums, you don't need anything. In the ghetto, nobody could stop three of you get together and stand up and sing.'

Return to R&B

When rock steady took over from ska and the emphasis shifted back to vocals, much of the effort put into creating a genuinely Jamaican musical form evaporated as the singers did their best to sound like their favourite Americans.

According to Byron Lee: 'The Blues Busters were simulating Sam and Dave, Jimmy Cliff was simulating Otis Redding, Bob Marley And The Wailers were a take off of Curtis Mayfield and The Impressions … when acts came on to do shows, they'd have to sing copy versions of songs by the act they were simulating as an introduction, only then, when they'd got the applause for that, could they do original material.'

Indeed, The Impressions made a huge impact on mid-1960s Jamaica, as they toured there frequently and their tight three-part harmonising became the role model for what became the Jamaican style of rock steady singing. Trios like The Melodians, The Techniques and The Paragons owed a great debt to Mayfield's group for their vocal style. The Wailers, however, went one step further and appropriated their style.

Ken Boothe and Freddie McGregor putting on the style in London. They have their own reasons for the dominance of Jamaican music over the last 40 years:

Ken: 'Because that was when we turned independ-ent and as an independent nation we get the courage and strength to do what we feel …'

Freddie: ' … and we feel creative, a creativity that has always come out in our singing. I am me, I'm free, I'm going to create something that is me. Totally new. This is Jamaica … Reggae … This is us.'

Ken: 'Yeah. Up front.'

Derrick Harriott on Rock Steady

'Rock steady was the most memorable time for Jamaican music, these songs can't die … they live on. Even in the era of dancehall they're always doing over the rock steady beat, they just put the dancehall feel to it.

'It changed from ska, really, because people just wanted a change. It's like a style of shirt, you don't want to wear the same style shirt all the time, you just want something different. The man who did most to make the change was Lyn Taitt, a guitarist who slow the beat down to about half the tempo of ska. He slow the tempo down on a tune called "Sound And Pressure", I think it was Hopeton Lewis, and that's where rock steady started because everybody wanted that beat. He work for Studio One, he work for Duke Reid, he work for independents like me, anybody who wanted that true rock steady feel. All the best rock steady tunes had Lyn Taitt playing guitar at the heart of them.

'Not that the fast beat died, it was still around there somewhere, but mostly it was rock steady in the dance, like them can't take that fast beat no more. The dances the people were doing was like to just bounce, you know, *rock steady*, and they loved it. But really they loved it for the singing, it was the beautiful singing and the melodies. Jamaicans are a people who love to sing – everybody sings, there's a church on every corner and people who go in them sing – and there was some singing in ska but not as much as now. These songs had a lot of vocals.

Derrick Harriott in his Kingston Store

'With rock steady what would happen at the dance was if the session just buck up and everything right then people would sing along loud and clear. Those songs had the good choruses and melodies, so the guy would start a tune off, then if it hitting tight he would turn the set off and leave everybody singing. That still went on for years later but it was created in the rock steady era, people sung with the song, they dance and sung along.'

4
forward the bass

Toots and the Maytals

Remarkably the word 'reggae' didn't make its first public appearance until 1968 when The Maytals put out the single 'Do The Reggay'. At the time it was a faddish new style that had a faster, tempo, but it had an enormous effect on both the music and the music business.

In terms of ages of Jamaican music, if ska was the birth and rock steady was its adolescence, the reggae era, the period around the end of the 1960s and the beginning of the 1970s, was the coming of age. After rock steady's very deliberate Americanisms – it was always, unabashedly, the island's take on the soul music of the day – the arrival of reggae represented a re-Jamaicanisation of the island's musical output with a far greater degree of nationalism than had been the case with ska. The new style also involved a far greater proportion of the country than previous developments, therefore spreading the industry much wider, allowing a far greater cross-section of the population to have access. And a great deal of this advancement was precipitated, in one way or another, by electricity.

Fundamentally, the change to reggae was triggered by the electric bass and the electric organ establishing themselves as vital to the way Jamaican music was made. The important thing

about the new bass wasn't so much that it was there – it had been for a few years – but that a new generation of players were exploring it and were eager to use it in its own right rather than simply try to imitate the acoustic stand-up model. As a result, the bass became almost aggressive in its moving up towards the front of the mix, a new-found buoyancy that rebalanced the standard rhythm section to form a relationship with the drums that would dictate reggae's directions for years to come. It was then, as the bass was becoming the foundation instrument, that songs started to get written on it, and it's no coincidence that since the end of the 1960s so many of the musical directors or arrangers in Jamaica have been bass players.

The electric organ may not have had such a lasting effect as the bass, but at the time it was no less crucial, as it clearly defined the lines between the new style and the previous one, thus effectively providing the catalyst for change.

Jimmy Cliff

The Pioneers

Once again it was a matter of approach, as the keyboards were being played with arched fingers to produce a stabbing, staccato line and, with it, the jerkiness associated with early reggae. A faulty electric organ at one of the prominent studios has been blamed for this percussive playing – apparently the keys would stick unless you hit them hard – and it's not a story I'm prepared to argue with. As such, the pattern could hardly have been further from the almost oily smooove of rock steady; it meant the new style was easily identified at whatever sound system was modern enough to start playing it and so could be seen to be catching on fast. A raise in tempo completed the stylistic removal, but that shift was actually one more example of a fine Jamaican tradition: once a style had dominated for a while, dancehall patrons demanded something new.

At the same time, affordable studio technology was advancing on an almost daily basis as solid-state equipment took over from the old valve set-ups. While this meant all sorts of rudimentary outboard gear was arriving at Jamaica's better studios, producing effects that enhanced this new sound – notably the echo that did much to define reggae's *skanga skanga* guitar lick – it also meant that a myriad of small studios were springing up. Effectively, this took the reins from those who had run t'ings for the past few years and handed them to a new level of producers and label owners, a lot of whom were musicians themselves, and, in the majority of cases, their prime concern was selling records rather than keeping their sound systems on top. The impact was felt immediately, as it meant a massive broadening of the scope of the ideas and aspirations that powered Jamaica's recording industry.

There was a sense of adventure about the music now that hadn't been seen since the jazz-steeped ska musicians used to try to cut each other to ribbons on the Kingston nightclub bandstands. In spite of rock steady's undeniable spirit and gleaming musical polish, as the reggae rhythms took over it became obvious that, in terms of sheer vitality, Jamaican music had been becalmed of late. Maybe that wasn't rock steady's fault, perhaps a style that is so dedicated to the art of singing simply didn't allow itself the room for too much madness. Reggae, however, was an entirely different matter – the basic framework was so strong that it could support virtually anything going on inside it and impose itself on any arrangement to facilitate cover-version heaven. Naturally, musicians loved this state of affairs and there was a distinct whiff of the *avant garde* about the first few years when reggae ruled the nation. Songs as odd and as varied as 'The Liquidator', 'Monkey Man', 'It Mek', 'Long Shot Kick de Bucket' and a version of 'The Theme From Shaft' could all call themselves reggae without worrying about the man from Trades Descriptions.

By 1971 it shifted its tempo and attitude but had remained very much reggae, accommodating the simmering anger of 'Trenchtown Rock', 'Maga Dog' and 'Let The Power Fall On I'. Yet it still found it within itself to cope with 'Mule Train' and 'Groovin' Out On Life'. In fact, all through that decade, reggae remained versatile enough to provide the fuel for roots' fires and the soft fluffy clouds on which floated lovers rock.

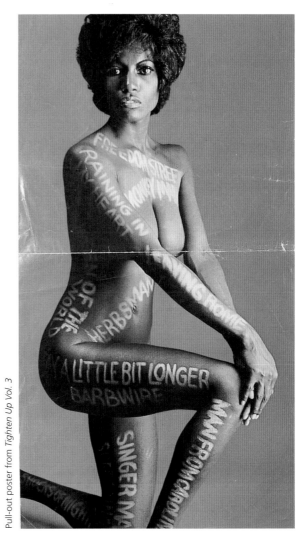

Pull-out poster from *Tighten Up Vol. 3*

Perhaps the main reason why reggae took such a hold of the Jamaican people, and why there was such an abundance of ideas within it, is because it passed the people's music back to the people. Once again, electricity played a part – in the immediately previous years, Jamaica had been progressively powering up its rural regions as the national grid reached more and more of the country. This meant a fresh exposure to music on jukeboxes in bars, on the radio and from touring shows such as Byron Lee's, but what had been lost in time was made up for in gusto. Country folk, keen to get involved in music, poured into the capital – the premise of the film *The Harder They Come* has its feet firmly planted in reality – and brought the country with

them in the form of different, rural-type sounds and more traditional Jamaican musical styles. Naturally, this had a huge effect on music that had, up until then, been a strictly urban situation. The overall sound became a more organic place to be, with many of the sounds used harking back to Africa, with Kumina and Burru percussion influences on display and in reggae's guitar patterns a distinct echo of mento's banjo. It was a far more inclusive approach, meaning the whole island could feel it was part of the music and so would take it far more seriously than what had gone before.

It was also when reggae went truly international. Whereas ska and rock steady hadn't reached too far past expat communities across the USA, Canada and the UK, as a structure that could support most styles, reggae gatecrashed the cosy world of British mainstream pop music by acquiring full orchestral arrangements. These lush string sections were added in England, on top of basic rhythm tracks that were made in Kingston and turned such bouncy reggae tunes as Bob & Marcia's 'Young, Gifted And Black' and Nicky Thomas's 'Love Of The Common People' into *bona fide* pop classics. This success opened the door for a lot more reggae – stringsed up and otherwise – to find its way into British homes of all persuasions and, as a side-effect, to find its way all over the world thanks to London being something of a tourist hub.

After putting all that work in, it's no wonder that reggae 'the style' ended defining reggae 'the genre', even though what might be called reggae now bears little relation to those popping organ lines or crisp guitar strokes.

Bob & Marcia in about 1969, a symphony in polyester.

Bob Andy

Dennis Brown

Sugar Minott Remembers Dennis Brown

Even three years after his death, Dennis Brown remains the best-loved reggae star in Jamaica. While nobody will doubt the respect and admiration there is for Bob Marley, he is seldom spoken about with the same open affection as Dennis Brown. The difference is that while Marley may have achieved more internationally, Dennis Brown never left the island and remained, first and foremost, of his own people. This may be ultimately what killed him.

A child star with a winning smile and beautiful tenor voice, Dennis Brown was one of the most-recorded singers in the industry – every producer wanted a D Brown record and he wasn't the sort of man who could say no. He seldom made a mistake in front of the mic, whether it was love songs or roots and culture, as reggae classics like 'Money In My Pocket', 'Wolves And Leopards', 'Well Without Water', 'Cassandra' and 'Here I Come' prove. But Dennis Brown was a man who loved to please, and as the demands on his talent got more and more, so it was in many parties' interests to keep him going, to make sure he stayed up for this show or that recording session. In 1999 the man who never smoked a spliff as a youth died of pneumonia, addicted to crack cocaine.

Sugar Minott, a fellow singer, remembers his long-time close friend:

'The first time I saw Dennis Brown was like when he was maybe seven or eight years old, appearing on television to win a *Nuggets For The Needy* show – that's a show that raises money for charity. He was singing a Derrick Harriott song, "Solomon", never had no record released or anything at that point. Dennis Brown had charisma then, because he came in his suit, a little boy in a suit and that was like a big thing for us kids, made him somebody to follow.

'After I get to know him, I used to go to his yard when he was about fourteen and play ping pong and whatever. He was a soul star, like a little Michael Jackson, always dressed nice, never drink, never smoke, nothing like that. He was like a prince and everybody know him, everywhere you go it's "Dennis … Dennis" and he have a smile for everybody. And he was born with that voice. Most kids have to break their voice, even as a young boy you never hear that squeaky sound on no Dennis Brown song.

'Jamaica loved Dennis Brown, he had the most number ones of any Jamaican singer, but it was more than just his songs, it was his personality. Whenever you hear Dennis Brown was fighting or licking down somebody or cussing off a crowd or being rude to an audience? When? Never! A lovely person, a king, always giving, never trouble

nobody. And his lyrical content, whether it a message song or a love song, anything he was writing about was always positive. Play me one Dennis Brown song that's about rubbish … none … not even one. He never do a song that do down the government or do down religion or do down white people.

'He sing patois too, maybe that's why he wasn't a big international star, but it's another reason why Jamaicans love him so. He was always with his people, where he was born down on Orange Street, Big Yard, he would still go back there. You could get close to him, where other artists might be like "I'm too busy" he would come and sit right there, no ego. Jamaican people love him so that when he was sick, towards the end, and he'd go on stage and couldn't sing they'd sing the songs for him, they wasn't like "Get off the stage" or booing, they were crying. People cried that he couldn't sing.

'It was like he was too nice, he want to do everything to please everybody, if he want to tell a man to get lost, he don't know how to say it. He just go along with things. When he have a problem with drugs, too many people would rather make money from him than say "Look, this guy needs help, let's cancel the thing." He don't say no to nobody, that was how he was. They encourage him, use the drugs as bait, and when he's on tour, he's away from the people that really love him. It was terrible, when he did his last tour in Brazil, rather than cancel the shows or try to go on without Dennis Brown, they had an ambulance by the stage waiting for him to drop down.'

Rude Boys

The second half of the 1960s were the rude boy years, when violence in the dancehall became commonplace and the musical community was split into support or condemnation for these young thugs who were terrorising communities with gangsterism and intimidation. 'Tougher Than Tough', 'Johnny Too Bad', 'Rudy Got Soul', 'Judge Dread', 'You Can't Win', 'On The Run (With A Gun)' were all examples of records made with the rude-boy wars as their subject matter. Bunny Lee, however, was well acquainted with the real thing:

'Up until them times, people in Jamaica was dealing with love. They wasn't dealing with no gun business and no knife and them type of things. Then things changed with the rude boy era and the knife become wicked in the dancehall. One of the men that changed it was Busby, the original rude boy.

'They used to call him Busby The Giant and Saturday High Priest, and he was a rude boy. When them guys are coming to the dance they'll kill you if they see you dressed in a three-piece suit. Them guys changed things, them just come in their shorts with no shirt, turn up back way and the girls all flock to them. They say it them the dance rock steady named for because they just come in to a dance, stand up and rock steady, don't do nothing and the girls are all around them. When they reach the dance the deejay have to play "Cry Tough" by Alton Ellis – "*Anything you can do I can do better, I'm the toughest …*"

'They coming in from Trenchtown, and they used to go from dance to dance in the area, maybe twenty dance in one Saturday night and every dance promoter have to pay them. Have to pay them or his dance mash up. It was a protection racket, which is big in Jamaica today and it start off then. It getting out of hand now, not only in the music business but in other business.

'Rude boys love music, they follow most singers and the music business, which is why there was so many records made about them, they was getting involved with the music business. It weren't so much that people was supporting them why these records made, and other producers and artists, like Prince Buster, want to prove they weren't scared, so they made the anti rude-boy records. The whole thing of violence in the dancehall and gangsters in the music business start with the rude boys.'

Bunny (right) in younger days

5
cultural time

Lee Perry

'Ten years of independence and what's it done for me?'

That was the question on the lips of so many youngsters at the beginning of the 1970s. Jamaica was in a deep social and economic mire as a result of independence and the political choices in the following years.

The only reason the British pulled out when they did was because there was absolutely nothing left to make any money out of: the sugar industry had collapsed when cheaper European beet sugar replaced Caribbean cane sugar; bauxite had been exploited to the max; and lucrative deals had been done with the big American hotel chains for prime North Coast real estate. All that was left to look forward to was high unemployment and increasing trade deficits. Then, the ill-advised, American-friendly economic policies instigated by the Jamaican Labour Party as they formed the first post-independence government brought hard times to the people in the shape of double-figure inflation, food shortages and a vastly under-resourced welfare system. The independence hangover was acute, and riots and civil unrest were by now commonplace as people simply weren't going to take any more. Naturally, such dissatisfaction was going to start to make its presence felt in the music of the day.

It was on the sound systems that the voices of roots and culture first began to be heard. As the 1960s rolled into the 1970s, the established Kingston studios were pouring out shiny pop music, a great deal of which was aimed at the other side of the Atlantic as the UK was the biggest single market for reggae. In the dancehall though, deejays could pick up the mic and talk about anything they liked, which was usually what was going on around them, how they felt about the world and the way it was treating them. There were no filters or censorship in the dancehall, so the genuine passion and anger of the deejays came through in such a way it moved the crowds and found enormous popular support – after all, this new generation of deejays was still part of the communities they performed in and everybody was feeling the same pressure. It was a *bona fide* movement, but to gain wider acceptance these political statements needed to get recorded so they could travel further than a couple of blocks in West Kingston. But this was never going to be

straightforward and in the end precipitated a massive shake-up in the way the business operated.

The previous kingpins of the Jamaican music business may have started off as rebels, but by now they'd become the establishment. Political music made by a bunch of kids wasn't on their agenda. But galloping technology and the spread of the Jamaican love affair with music had led to a proliferation of small studios opening in the capital, and it was no longer necessary for anybody with ideas to go cap in hand to one of the big boys. These new studios were owned and operated by a second generation of producers who were either musicians and singers of the ska and rock steady days, who had learned enough from being around places like Studio One or Beverley's and wanted to do it for themselves, or they were the artists' contemporaries, who shared the same worldview and wanted to use their entrepreneurial abilities to promote change. This influx of new blood revolutionised the music as well as the music business. These producers felt no allegiance to the past and were much more willing to experiment and move things forward. By giving freer access to recording than had previously existed, they also opened up reggae to many more participants.

This allowed the whole tone of reggae to change. To replace the happy, chirpy stuff that had been going on before the rhythms slowed, basslines became more pronounced, noticeable east-Africanisms began to creep in, dub versions seemed to seek to intimidate with the very weight of their presence and lyrics pulled few punches as

The Mighty Diamonds

they told of society's ills and preached revolution. They also contained serious spirituality as Rastafari began openly to get involved in this new music.

Rasta had been in the background as long as there'd been a music business, but given the social climate of 1960s Jamaica, it didn't show itself – the majority of The Skatalites were Rasta, but they didn't grow dreadlocks because a) they wouldn't have got work anywhere, even in many of the studios; and b) it would have left them open for police persecution. The release of the film *The Harder They Come* provided much of the catalyst for Rasta going overground. This was the first time that it was possible to see images of dreads and sufferation on the big screen and this gave Rasta considerable legitimacy. In 1972, Michael Manley's left-wing People's National Party government came into power and was openly supportive of Rastafari, thus it became more acceptable to wear locks or red, green and gold in daily life. The effect on the music industry was an explosion of dread, as flashing locks during a performance became almost regulation. Rasta imagery and lyricism came to dominate reggae for the best part of a decade, creating some beautiful and apparently purposeful music. The biblical and spiritual messages, which were frequently words of war, seemed to spur Jamaican songwriters to previously unimaginable poetic heights, while the music and recording techniques were at their most inventive, matching the mood note for note. The roots period was a time when Jamaican music was taking on the world on its own terms, and the successes of Bob Marley, Culture, The Mighty Diamonds, Burning Spear,

Dennis Brown, Big Youth and Lee Perry were proof of what such internal harmony had achieved.

In spite of roots reggae's best efforts, economic conditions worsened under that PNP government and it was in the ghettos that this was felt the hardest in terms of unemployment and social decline. Initially, this boosted the spread of Rastafari in the inner city, as, quite apart from the escalating frustration, such disenfranchisement presented the ideal environment. Renouncing all things Babylonian is going to be a great deal easier if you don't have too much Babylonian to renounce, then, of course, if you've got time on your hands you've got so much more opportunity to praise Jah Jah. In fact, it's not unusual for old-time Rastas to tell you it was somehow divine that circumstances conspired to prevent them from working and therefore be able to devote themselves to all things spiritual

But although roots and culture seemed to make so much social sense and appeared to be strong as both a movement and a music, as reggae moved into the 1980s it just sort of disappeared. Yes, Bob Marley's death had some effect, but in terms of the music business and social influence, that was felt much harder off the island. The truth of the matter was that roots and culture had been falling apart for two or three years before Marley died and, ironically, this collapse was for the same reasons that it had come about in the first place. Teenage kids who'd grown up with it but had seen conditions around them decline were asking the very pertinent question, 'Ten years of roots and culture and what's it done for me?'

Lee 'Scratch' Perry

'Scratch is crazy. Totally crazy. And he produced some crazy music that I wasn't really satisfied with. I wasn't used to that kind of stuff … all that flanging, that space sound. It wasn't my kind of thing. I like clean arrangements, and some of those arrangements sound like them awful.'

Leroy Sibbles of The Heptones and formerly Studio One's musical director. Scratch produced the group's *Party Time* album

'He was very dramatic in the studio, behind the glass directing the session with body language, with hand movements and foot movements. He'd suggest things to us that seemed ridiculous, but we'd do them and then when we listen to it all back it all fits, like a jigsaw. That's Lee Perry, he doesn't have to have a reason. Lee Perry doesn't have to understand it. Lee Perry just does it. He's the Salvador Dali of reggae music.'

Ibo Cooper of Third World. He played on Bob Marley's Perry-produced *Punky Reggae Party*

'He was like a whirlwind in the studio, quite erratic actually. But to me Lee Perry is the Ennio Morricone of Jamaican music. He's that influential, and I think it's only now people are beginning to realise that.'

Paul Simonon of The Clash. Scratch mixed their 1977 single 'Complete Control'

'Scratch back then is a different Scratch to now. He had his sort of zany ways but he was also more down to earth and concentrated on the music side of things. He was somebody you could talk to in the studio, he would listen if you pointed things out to him and whatever idea you had he would build on it until it became something fantastic. But he was funny too. Scratch would draw up in his car, jump out, well dressed, and walk into the shop or the bar and someone would shout "Scratch, your car is down the road, man!" He would have forgotten to pull the brake up and he'd have to run to catch the darn car!'

Dave Barker, who was produced by Scratch as a solo artist before he became half of Dave & Ansel Collins

'Crazy. He was totally nuts. When it's mixing time nobody goes near the studio. He'd lock himself in for a couple of days … two … three days. He doesn't answer no phone, he doesn't answer no ringing of no bell, no beeper, no knock, *nothing*! Pauline, who at the time was his woman, she knows when he's hungry, so she knows when to go with food, but if you are there you can't see him because he's in his lab. He's a professor at work in his lab.

'He'd make music out of anything. Scratch takes an empty quart bottle and he throws in some water, knocks it *bip bip, bip* and gets one note and dubs that on to the tape. Then he puts some more water in and knocks it *bip bip bip* and gets a different sound, and put that on a different track on the tape. And so on. By the time he's filled the bottle he's got five different sounds on five different tracks, then he mixes them into one and he's got something he can use. The guy's a genius.

'Being with Lee Perry as a producer was actually the high point of my career. We had fun … I mean *we had fun*. And you can hear that fun on the album *War Ina Babylon*. Every time I hear the name Lee Perry I feel happy.'

Max Romeo, Scratch produced his seminal 1976 album *War Ina Babylon*

'I remember The Soulettes – my first group – recording a song with him called "Roast Duck". Everybody thought we were crazy, but we had to do this for Lee, to give him a chance because he gives so many people chances. He took the band in to Coxsone's studio and he did this song where he would say "*I want roast duck, I want roast duck …*" Then he took it to the sound systems and people like it, Lee Perry's song became a hit. So the next stage show we had, he was billed on the show and he ask us to come and do the background vocals.

'I was never so embarrassed in my life! They throw us off stage because Lee Perry is not a singer – there we are and he there, out front, with "*Ya, ya, ya, ya … they send me wild roast duck*!" Poor thing. And we was there saying "*Wa, wa, wa, roast duck*!" and singing. They boo and then the beer bottles start come over, and we had to go back on stage next with The Wailers! I was so embarrassed I said no, I would never go back on stage!'

Rita Marley

Lee Perry on Himself

'The secret from the sphinx is on my head, and this is the secret the sphinx have to tell you, that I am the IMF now and the father of the nation forever … Father Christmas. This is the return of Father Christmas with his magic mushroom.

'I've got everything. Mick Jagger making a mistake when he say God give him everything. God did not give Mick Jagger everything, God give I everything. He give me a wife and he give me all the money. All the American dollars, all the Irish pounds and all. And I have so much.

'I think I should come to London where my fans love me so much, where I know that English education is the best education in the universe. If you understand English words, you can go anywhere and take over the mind of people who are not educated and educate them with English words who are the proper language. The German language is nothing, but they have a good heart, but when you know English then you can teach your friend. In this world you go nowhere without a teacher or without a lamp. Follow the light and BBC and hip hop and reggae forever.

'I am the original rah from Egypt and I was there from the time when God give wonderful, beautiful Egypt for his people. Then I am Moses. I am Moses! I am Moses! I am Moses! Where is my rod? Here is my rod. Lightning is on my head. He didn't die, he disappear in a ball of fire and then he come again to hurt the people. He warn you, if you fight against ganja Rastafari I let you suffer, but I won't let you die. Until you know I'm ganja, then I will set you free.'

Lee Perry at work (above) in the studio and at play (left)
sightseeing in London on an open-topped bus

Burning Spear

Second to Bob Marley, Burning Spear probably has the biggest worldwide following of all reggae artists. He has done since he started extensive touring in the mid-1970s, and he's always been aware of acute differences between the Jamaican and the international reggae markets.

What are the main differences?

'It's in terms of listeners, in the international market people will be listening for music with quality, music with understanding, music wherein they could gain something from, music that could become a help in their life or lifestyle of living. That's the international section for reggae music, but back in Jamaica it's not like that, here people intend to listen more to gimmicks. No disrespect, but people don't care whether they're listening to something wherein they wouldn't gain anything or learn anything from, other than feeling happy or good. It's totally different.

'The people in the international music scene became a part of the music, you know, they programmed themselves to become a part of the music. On the Jamaica side, people don't care about being part of the music, and that's two big differences. I prefer people who listen and end up being part of what they are listening to, for it create a lot of strength and more confidence in myself and I know that what I'm doing is the right thing.'

Is that why you take your lyrics so seriously?

'I believe lyrics are very important. When you are putting a sound together you have to have your lyrics as clean as possible and carrying a lot of understanding. It's like you're telling a story, so therefore the listeners have a start, they have a middle and they have an end. It's to do with heart … you're gonna pay the heart, so are you gonna do the heart? Because someone gonna look at the heart and can they identify what the heart looking like or what the heart should be? They should have to.

'So you have to put those lyrics together so that people listening have something to follow. It's not like they're listening and run off the track, you have to stay on the track.'

Are lyrics perhaps less important to today's artists?

'For them it's varied. You know, for some time I don't know how some artist might be thinking when putting a song together, I know how *I'm* thinking when I'm putting a song together, but I can't tell you how they're thinking.'

Perry Henzell

'*The Harder They Come* is the big city seen through the eyes of a country boy, it's really the story of an illusion. The promise of the city was a very cruel illusion, because somebody like Ivan coming to the big city has been filled full of "you can get it if you really want", but the fact is you *can't* get it if you really want. No matter how hard you try. Unless you have some education ... unless you have some discipline ... unless you have some connections ... unless ... a dream will not see you through.

'About that time, huge quantities of youngsters were coming in from the countryside, in Jamaica, in Rio, in Jakarta, in Johannesburg, all over. They were flooding into the city, brought by the promise of the transistor radio, which was beaming that dream into the countryside for the first time in history. And they were arriving in the cities with a dream. The theme of *The Harder They Come* is that they would rather die than give up that dream. They would rather they died than they killed that dream. I think the real message of *The Harder They Come* has been hugely misunderstood.'

Perry Henzell, writer, producer and director of *The Harder They Come*

Joe Higgs: the man who inspired the embryonic Wailers

Max Romeo on the Rise of Rasta

Although Rastafari had existed in Jamaica since the 1930s, and had staked its claim in the modern music business for as long as there was a modern music business – Don Drummond, Lloyd Brevett and several other Skatalites were Rastas – it wasn't until the 1970s that the movement went above ground. Although they were still persecuted and discriminated against in many aspects of life, Jamaicans began wearing dreadlocks openly and Rasta camps and meeting places were no longer routinely destroyed by the police and soldiers. One of the reasons for this rise in Rasta was the way life had turned out for ordinary Jamaicans during the ten or so years since independence and that Rasta offered a cohesive sense of rebellion and a way of living that made more sense. But that doesn't really explain the new openness that encouraged Big Youth to flash his locks on stage at the Carib Theatre one evening and for the previously afro'd Wailers to start locksing up. After all, the previous generation of Rastafarian musicians would never have dreamed of – dared to? – throwing the comb away. Max Romeo, reckons this change of attitude was down to Rasta's old adversary, politics.

'When I and I put politics together from ancient times, it mean people's parasite. Poli means people and tics is a parasite so when you put it together it's people's parasite and I and I is aware of the fact that these guys are parasites, so we try to distance ourselves from them. That's why we aren't into politics *per se*, but we follow Michael Manley, me and a few other artists.

'At the time, we were dealing with what you would call capitalism and the island was being controlled by sixteen families owning three-quarters of the wealth, while the other quarter share among the rest of us, the millions of … peasants. Michael Manley come to change that, so we say "Yeah" and we agree with his concept. But, importantly, he liberate Rasta. It's because of Michael Manley that I, as a Rasta, can go into any establishment in Jamaica and I can work in any job in Jamaica. Before Michael Manley, Rasta have to hide, because if the soldier or policeman catch us they trim us – cut off our dreadlocks – and we don't want them trim us, they will kill us.

'He stand up for the poor and say give the poor man a chance. He know that Rasta is just ordinary Jamaicans who is trying to live good and honestly even if that make them poor, so he want to give them a chance, get them involved. That's why so many see it was safe to wear locks and praise Jah and still be part of Jamaican society, because he made it so. I and I owe Michael Manley respect for that, but it wasn't actually *per se* Rasta involved with politics. Rasta don't mix with politics, I and I don't mix with parasites. Period.'

Max Romeo at home in Kingston with his family

Augustus Pablo

Politics and Music

'Music plays an important role in Jamaican politics,' explains Edward Seaga, leader of the Jamaican Labour Party. 'All our public meetings and street rallies are punctuated with music. Music and politics have been fairly comfortable bedfellows since the island had its first free elections 40 years ago. You couldn't have just speeches. These are street things, not town-hall things, and you couldn't have just a consecutive run of speeches – it would be boring because it would be four or five hours and people are just standing there. So it has to be punctuated, and after each speaker there's a musical interlude. Not just a performer but by the people themselves singing.'

Although this relationship was something that came to prominence during the roots and culture time, tunes like 'They Got To Go', 'Help The Weak', 'Carry Go Bring Come' place social comment songs back as far as the ska days. In fact, before then when music was seen as such a potent election weapon it was banned.

'It's very significant that our first set of election laws prohibited the use of live entertainment during election campaigns,' PJ Patterson, leader of the People's National Party, points out, 'because it was felt that music could sway the crowd one way or another. We have since abolished that rule as being totally obsolete. People must be allowed to express themselves and musicians express the feelings of the people, they reflect the mood of the people.

'It's fair to say,' he goes on, 'that while the political situation influences music, it also works the other way around and the music influences the political situation. Both the music and the culture interact upon each other and with each other.'

The unique relationship between music and politics on the island is one of the very few areas that Patterson and Seaga, Prime Minister and Leader of the Opposition, agree on. But this isn't too surprising, they both have music business backgrounds, Patterson used to manage The Skatalites and Seaga was one of Jamaica's first record producers. The first music to be used at political rallies drew heavily on Jamaica's church traditions and the songs were straight appropriations of rousing religious choruses with the name of whatever politician being lauded substituted for that of Jesus or whoever. The fashion didn't last very long, as it became much simpler and more popular to adopt music of the day and take one song as a campaign theme song. Not that this can't get you into trouble, as Patterson remembers.

'In 1980 there was a Bob Marley tune called "A Bad Card" and both parties were playing that tune. So you'd be travelling through the country-side and you'd hear the tune coming to you from across the valley or out of the hills but until you got in sight you wouldn't know if it was your campaign team or a hostile campaign team.'

Perhaps the most famous campaign song is Delroy Wilson's 'Better Must Come', a PNP anthem that, according to Patterson, 'drove the Michael Manley government from the very first day of its election to do everything possible to improve the social conditions and the economic welfare of the people of Jamaica.

6
the tuffest of the tuff

What really marked The Wailers out as being a cut above the other singing groups of the day wasn't, necessarily, their ability but the fact they could transcend it. They always achieved far more than the sum of their parts, as what they were looking for in their songwriting and vocal expression pushed reggae forward.

Not shackled by rock steady/early reggae's love-song conventions, The Wailers were writing conscious lyrics from way back in their lives, their brand of soul singing was exactly that – singing from the soul instead of merely singing soul songs. It forced them to push each other with a creative friction that can only exist in a unit as tight as they were, and produced the best from each of them. When they hit it right with the right song to get them going, Bob Marley's raw emotion, Bunny Livingston's upper register and Peter Tosh's tenor combined to offer up an awesome taste of what The Wailers were capable of as a group.

It was in their very act of taking reggae's parameters more than just a little bit further that their importance lies; while they weren't by any means the first to write or record conscious songs, their approach and breadth of lyricism showed there was another way. That is, if rock steady's song structures don't fit rebel music's attitude then don't use them, and the imaginative use of metaphor shouldn't be a

federal offence. Likewise their musical phrasing and dense, Lee Perry-style arrangements offered an alternative approach to a tune that allowed in other influences and better reflected the evolving local music scene. Oddly, while The Wailers stretched the boundaries of reggae music, they were rarely imitated; they were more a spiritual than a tangible influence. However, it was this more adventurous approach to their craft that made it very easy for the rest of the world to get a grip on them. That and the fact that their powerful soul style communicated itself across a greater distance than the more conventional Jamaican ways with a song that relied on, if not previous knowledge, then at least a prior understanding.

There is no doubt that a great deal went missing when that threesome went their separate ways, as not only were the harmonies completely in tune with each other – emotionally as well as musically – but the edge of tension that three very strong individuals brought to the table was never really recaptured.

And any sense of regret is made more so when you look at what the other two actually achieved post-Wailers: Peter made a handful of fantastic singles, but even his mum would've been stretched to play one of his albums all the way though, and he'd perform stage shows that veered wildly from the fiercely quirky to the borderline idiotic; Bunny was always going to struggle to live up to his sublime first solo album, *Blackheart Man*, and he never even came close. In both cases there was/is a feeling that neither has ever lived up to the potential they showed as part of the threesome.

Bob, too, suffered artistically as, with few exceptions, all his best songs were written during The Wailers years, and it's impossible to say if he lived up to his potential as far as songs went. This is because no reggae act had ever got this big, thus pretty much everything was a bonus. Also, any notion of 'could've-done-better' is balanced by the astonishing level even his substandard songs reached and the notion that far fewer people would have got to hear them had the group remained together. And that is what is vital to the Bob Marley story, as any 'potential' he might have had very quickly transcended the merely musical. Since Marcus Garvey, no Jamaican had assumed such a world platform, and you could question whether Garvey was as influential as Bob Marley. The Third World had never produced a global superstar: in his dress code, hairstyle, drug habits, speech patterns, Bob Marley impacted on his audience in far more ways than merely musical.

Did he reach his potential? Probably not. Just after Marley died, in May 1981, it was announced in sections of the media that this marked the end of reggae. But that was never ever true. His death didn't mark the end of roots reggae – that had been happening without any outside help for a number of years. Bob Marley's death didn't even mark the end of the star himself, as his records have sold in far greater numbers since his death, and the iconic status Marley now occupies in America is something that's come about in the past 20 years.

In Jamaica, reggae had been moving on steadily for the last decade or so of Marley's life and although he was to be profoundly missed as a Jamaican popular hero – probably the most popular and the most heroic in the island's recent memory – the music closed up around any hole without so much as a ripple. What it marked was the end of an era in which reggae was a *bona fide* part of mainstream music, occupying its own space on its own terms. This wasn't because people had stopped liking the music – the public at large continues to want to like reggae and to want that reggae to be the real deal – it was because there was no subsequent focus for attention that fulfilled all criteria as completely as Bob Marley. Nobody who was genuinely able to straddle the almost mutually exclusive worlds of credible roots reggae and conventional rock superstardom.

The interesting aspect of the mainstream's reaction to Bob Marley's death is in the brief but intensive search for 'The Next Bob Marley' that happened during the first few years of the 1980s. Any vaguely charismatic dread was being groomed for the position. It's actually something that still goes on today and it's not even worth discussing who has or who has not been put forward for the job – even those who share Bob's surname – because the notion that anybody could replace him simply speaks volumes about those who spent time on such a quest. To look for another Bob Marley shows you never really *got* the first one. How he, Peter and Bunny arrived on the radar in the first place is precisely because they did it outside of the conventional music business. The Zippo lighter album with the rock-friendly overdubs may be the popular choice as the group's starting point, but the next one, *Burnin'*, was raw Wailers and the one the public bought, just as the Lee Perry sessions recorded prior to *Catch A Fire* are still acclaimed as their best work.

Why the world listened to Bob Marley was because he remained unadulterated by the business he chose to operate in. He made the impression he did because, while he may have chosen rock music as his conduit and taken advantage of a few of its benefits, that was as far as he went with it and what he delivered was pure Trenchtown. Right up until he died. He never tried to be anything or anybody else, and thus remained in total control of who he was and what he did, and nobody else can do that, no matter how much record industry grooming they receive. Unsurprisingly, none of these 'New Bob Marley's' made it out of the gate. You'd think there'd be a lesson in that, wouldn't you?

It's impossible to underestimate the importance of The Wailers in the story of reggae. Yet, and it's one more of those typically Jamaican apparent paradoxes, had they not existed there would have been no need to invent them. Creatively, reggae would have developed along the same lines as it has done anyway, but far fewer people would have taken it so seriously.

Bob Marley by Those Who Knew Him

'Women throwing themselves at Bob was part of the business. I thought that it was natural. It wasn't really hurtful, but it was something I had to reckon with. I had to be very intelligent. I couldn't take it like a housewife, I had to take it like one who works with this man and one who has his children and one who takes her career serious. I wasn't going to lose my position because of my husband's lifestyle.

'I knew we had love. So much of a perfect love that we would have to be careful what we're going to let break this thing apart. And if there's something that we can do to help this, we're going to do it. Cos this was meant to be. And I was able to say yes to each child when they were born. He'd say "Rita, you know this girl have this baby, or this girl say she pregnant. What do you think?" It was always about how I think, so we develop a sort of a brother-sister relationship at some point where I just couldn't be the jealous wife. I had my feelings but I had to be in control of them to save the day … to save the relationship.

'With much of it, we know it's a one-night stand – some of them doesn't even come on the

bus. As long as they don't sleep over. At the end of the day, he's mine, I'm his.'
Rita Marley, Bob's wife and backing singer

'I thought at the time they were one of the greatest things I ever listened to. They had great, great harmonies – they were sweet with Bunny all the way up top and Peter in the middle there and Bob out front being so strong and soulful. They had it going on too, they had it all. They knew what they were, what they were doing and where they were heading. They had their concept.'
Leroy Sibbles of The Heptones

'Bob was very quiet. Bob hardly spoke. He was more a rude-boy type of guy and nobody really confronted Bob in any shape or form. But he was a sociable, easy-going person, and even though he didn't talk much you knew that you and him were on a certain level. Peter didn't appear to talk at all. Sometimes we would pass each other going to the studio or on the road and the only thing that came from Peter if I said, "Yes Peter", he would answer back, "Yes Irie" and that's it. Bunny was quite sociable though. The most talkative of them all.'
Dave Barker who sang on The Wailers'
Lee Perry sessions before he became half
of Dave & Ansel Collins

'Bob was a very regimented person. When we were on tour, when we finished working, when we come off the stage at night, Bob would call us into his room, wearing our nightclothes and he would have

a song that he's writing and he wants harmonies. He would rehearse us over and over again, but I see that it produced perfection, he was a perfectionist. When you were working with Bob you could sing like you're in a backyard or in your living room because that's how he made you feel when you'd finished working. Because you do it over and over, you know it so much that you have so much confidence in singing that song.

'He was a disciplinarian too. He was the first to be on the bus when we are on tour. It didn't matter what time we were leaving, even if we were leaving out at night, when you got down Bob would already be on the bus. Sometimes you might get down about ten or fifteen minutes late, and he'd be there. He wouldn't actually say anything to you, but just by his being there he'd be saying: "Hey, I'm here, you need to follow my example." He was a true leader.'
Judy Mowatt of The I-Threes, The Wailers'
backing singers

'I was Miss World when I began my relationship with Bob, and as Miss World you're like an employee, you have a job to do for a year and that means fulfilling engagements as an international beauty queen. It was a big step for Bob, a Rasta, to get involved with someone like me, and there was no doing it quietly. I didn't even realise how much it impacted on his life and he took as much flak about it as I did from my uptown set. When I was with Bob or would be seen with him, I used to try my hardest to always have on a long skirt, have my hair covered, have my face scrubbed clean of

Bob Marley and the Wailers on the Old Grey Whistle Test in 1973

make-up, no nail polish. None of the things that were considered forbidden when we were in a certain set of circumstances.

'When I used to go back to the house in Oakley Street, London, where he was staying, I used to take it all off before I got back there. I would be in a train coming in from God knows where and you know the size of the bathrooms on trains? There's this little sink that can fit in the palm of your hand and the water is

ice cold and I'm in there cleaning off this make-up so when I do get back to the house nobody's going to frown the minute I walk in through the door. You know, "Who is the painted doll?"

'I can remember one night though, coming in and I didn't have the chance to remove it before-hand. And no sooner had I stepped through the front door, full regalia, the gown, the fur, the hair, the makeup … everything, than he stepped in right behind me. I spun around, he just looked me up and down, real slow, and burst out laughing. Him say: "I catch you!"'

Cindy Breakspeare, former Miss World and mother of Damian Marley

'Bob was a very disciplined, determined man. If Bob have to say this leaf have to stay here on the ground under this tree, he will do anything to make sure the leaf stay here. He's a man like that. He believe in what he is doing, which is very important, but you have to believe in yourself to believe in what you are doing. If he saw other people really trying to do something he would be encouraging, a lot of strong encouragement, a lot of beautiful encouragement. Which is also very important. You know when one can identify you doing something, you try to do something, that's where you need the help. He was there to strength your encouragement, to tell you to go ahead. That you are doing the right thing, continue to do the right thing.'

Burning Spear

'Apart from music, football was everything to Bob Marley, after music it was his first love. Anywhere he went, he always carried a soccer ball, he had a ball in his car. He went into a hotel, the first thing is he checks in then the ball comes out. In the suites he's juggling the ball while he talked to people, all the time. In the early days, we used to pay a lot of unnecessary bills because he'd be trying to control the ball and hit glass and things. Because, back then, he wasn't all that polished a player, he was a little bit wild. But eventually, after a year or two, we managed to get that touch together and he became a very good player, good control and could handle himself. We didn't break things any more!

'Football helped him, it helped him with his music and his touring as it got him in good condition – good physical condition and get the mind together too.'

Allan 'Skill' Cole, Bob Marley's manager, best friend and Jamaica's best-ever professional footballer

'I met Bob under very unusual circumstances because he was married to my sister, so the relationship between Bob Marley and myself was like I'd have with an older brother. But I was around him so much that I was able to see the way he interacted with other people. People knew the power this man had, and to be with him in a room and to see the way people behaved around him was amazing. They were like small children when they were introduced to Bob or when they were in his presence. Sometimes he'd be very stern with them, you know, very presidential and another time he'd be the real joker, teasing people or cajoling them to come out and play football.

'On top of that, he was a very caring type of person. If there was one meal cooked and there was ten people there and enough food for eight he'd let everyone eat bar him. He was that type of person, he would let everybody eat first. He had a fatherlike feeling for everybody.'

The Ranking Miss P, BBC radio deejay and sister of Rita Marley

The I-Threes as they are today: Judy Mowatt (above left) in the hills above Kingston; Rita Marley (above) at the Bob Marley Museum and Marcia Griffiths (right) at home in Miami

Left: Bob Marley and friend at Regine's nightclub in Paris, 1977

Below: Ranking Miss P, BBC Radio deejay and Bob Marley's sister-in-law

Above: Allan 'Skill' Cole: Jamaica's greatest footballer and Marley's best mate

Left: Bob Marley with Tony 'Gillie' Gilbert on the tour bus during the Exodus tour of Europe

Bunny Wailer

Sitting in the First Street yard where, 40 years ago, The Wailers used to meet and practise their harmonies, Bunny Wailer looks back on those early days.

'Trenchtown is totally different now compared to what it was in the fifties, sixties and seventies … even coming into the eighties. Since then, the political terrorism has spoiled a lot of communities. Life used to be worth living in places like Trenchtown, so when we, The Wailers, started it was vibrant with a lot of activities. People going to and fro, to school, to work, to play, you would find the streets crammed with people.

'People from other communities would come here because they'd want to acquaint themselves with the many talents that were in Trenchtown. In those times, there were so many activities, such a vibrancy, and music was at the centre of that. Trenchtown was like Piccadilly … it was like Hollywood.

'My father and Bob's mother had a child so we share a sister, which was a bond between us even before any music came into it so we grew up as brothers. We met Peter in Trenchtown. He had migrated from his parish down in Westmoreland to come to Trenchtown to be an electrical welder, just like Bob trained to be a welder when he started singing at Beverley's. Although in the beginning we were all focussing on solo careers, we still wanted to have a group because groups at the time were swinging and those harmones were creating excitement. Also it would have been kind of lonely out there as a solo act, as a group we could learn from each other, we could grow with more confidence.

'That was important for us, because we were youth, growing up to be professional people in other areas and we really walked away from a lot of responsible duties to be entertainers. Bob was training to be a welder, Peter too, and I was in school getting ready to go to university. Our parents were really concerned because we were still teenagers and still under our parents' rule and control.

'At that time, it was five parts because we started as a five member group, with myself, Bob, Peter, Junior Braithwaite and Beverly Kelso. So we were listening to five-member groups like The Platters, The Drifters, Little Anthony And The Imperials, but when we went down to three members, The Impressions were our choice. They were really impressive in their style, and The Wailers had a similar kind of harmonic style, so we kinda got linked with Curtis Mayfield and The Impressions in that respect.

'Once we got going as a trio, we started to change our voices. We can all sing high tenor, we can all sing bass. You could never know if it is me or Peter singing, I'd have to tell you that it was me doing that part or Peter was doing that part – sometimes I would start with the bass and end up with high tenor, Peter the same. We'd shift around all the time, and that's what made The Wailers different from the rest of the groups. Also, because The Wailers were so locked in harmony you could not identify the individual unless they went into the lead.

'It was a lot of hard work, but we listened and learned from Joe Higgs and that is what made the trio so strong.'

7
toasters, boasters and righteous preachers

Dr Alimentado

It is said that without Jamaican deejays there would be no rap – or not as we know it. Whether this is true or not it sells Jamaican deejays and deejay culture short as it implies that what occurred on the island's sound systems was little more than embryonic.

The art of deejaying, Jamaican style, has covered far more ground than its American counterpart hip-hop. Even taking into account that it's been around roughly twice as long, in terms of influence on both music and the world, it's left a far more vivid impression. The way the hip hop connection came about has a particularly Jamaican flavour, in that something was taken onto the island, adapted to suit a Jamaican purpose and then re-introduced to the world in a far more interesting form. The notion of bigging up a deejay's sound system was, originally, 'borrowed' from across the Gulf of Mexico as an approximation of the Southern American black radio jocks' scat-style station identifications and their almost palpable excitement at playing certain records – soul star Rufus Thomas was one of the best. However, once this unofficial American import had served a few years in Jamaica, it had evolved to such a degree that it was adopted back into black American culture as rap. What had happened was that an art form that, in the first place, was all about showing off had rubbed up

against Jamaican macho and all the usually endearing elements stuck – it's perpetually witty, constantly quick on its feet, has a keenly developed sense of self, takes no prisoners in the battle of the sexes, is remorselessly competitive and has a logic about it that may not be immediately apparent but falls into place eventually. All the ingredients of early rap.

So it's really little wonder that when it was shipped back to America in the 1970s, courtesy of Jamaican expat sound system owner DJ Kool Herc, it was so attractive and easily absorbed. But as appealing as this off-the-peg attitude was, it wasn't what turned radio scatting into rap as we know it. The most significant development that had taken place on deejay's Jamaican sojourn was its new function: thanks to the likes of U-Roy, Scotty and Dennis Alcapone it had moved from being in-between the records or even over the top of the records to actually being part of them. The deejays no longer had to service the stars, they *were* the stars. Officially.

Prince Jazzbo: A Study in Cool

Prince Far-I

To understand fully what the Jamaican deejay means, you have to understand exactly what the Jamaican deejay is and how far removed they are from a) the radio deejay and their endless stream of inane patter; or b) the club deejay who never seems quite as big as their record box. The Jamaican deejay doesn't just introduce the music, or play the music, or even select the music, in many cases they *are* the music. And a great deal more besides. Quite apart from simply dominating the Jamaican recording industry for the past couple of decades, deejays have dictated broad-brush changes to the music, heralded new approaches to life on the island, proved powerful political influences, and kept much of the population up to speed with what's going on. It's not for nothing Jamaica's deejays were called 'the ghetto's newspaper' (more recently, thanks to

Public Enemy's Chuck D, 'the ghetto's CNN'), although even that's an understatement. They didn't just report the news, they shaped it, commented on it, delivered it in such a way it would have an effect on their listeners, explained it, invited reaction and incited their audiences to do something about it. It won't surprise anybody to learn that Gil Scott-Heron's dad is Jamaican.

Deejays such as Big Youth, Tappa Zukie, Prince Far-I, I-Roy and a later model U-Roy were responsible for ushering in the roots'n'culture era. On Kingston's sound systems, they were decrying what was being done to their country and running an effective recruitment campaign for Rastafari long before anything significant made it onto record. The deejay had been, by then, boosted practically to griot (West African praise-singer) status, which was a mark of how swiftly they had adapted to and grown into their roles. Spearheading the idea of reggae as a rebel music was really just an expansion of what they'd always done in the dancehalls but now they were doing it on a national scale. It's a big part of the uniqueness of Jamaican deejays that they could do this. Their art form has always been instant – what made a good deejay was his ability to rhyme on the spot, to improvise and talk about whatever he wanted to or what had just popped into his head. To react quickly, whatever the environment.

Looking back, though, it seems obvious it should have been the deejays who led the charge into roots'n'culture: they had the means, the ability and the people's ear. What they also had was excitement. Very often, the worthiness factor involved in this era of reggae precludes how exciting it was to watch somebody such as Big Youth whipping off his tam to flash his dreadlocks to a crowd, or the physically imposing Prince Far-I denouncing Rome in his portentous gravel voice, or ex-civil servant I-Roy lacing his tales of sufferation with the blackest of humour. Yet that was what deejays did – they excited their crowds. In fact, for the past 40 years they've consistently been the most obviously exciting and appealing aspect of Jamaican music. Outside of any responsibilities they assumed during the roots-reggae era, that was the extent of their job description – to be exciting. Way back in the early days of the big sound systems, Prince Buster and Coxsone employed guys like King Stitt and Count Machuki for no other reason than to vibe up their set. It wasn't rocket science: the better the deejay, the better the crowd and the better the take at the bar. What they did was all about charisma and showmanship, a tradition that continued through U-Roy and Dennis Alcapone and Dillinger to the roots deejays. Big Youth, Tappa Zukie, Trinity and Prince Jazzbo may have had plenty to say, but they never let that get in the way of their performances. After all, they kept the cauldron of social discontent simmering for around a decade and couldn't have done that if they'd been boring.

When reggae entered the dancehall era, post roots'n'culture, of course it was the deejays that took it there – the music had to come back into popular control and that meant sound systems and deejays. What was less predictable, however, was the deejays' domination that has been such a feature of reggae since the 1980s. This has an

Dillinger

enormous amount to do with that same excitement factor; after all, whether or not you agree with much of what dancehall appears to go out of its way to represent, you'd have to be clinically dead not to be moved by dancehall deejays' inherent excitement quota.

Take Yellowman, for example, who in so many ways sums up what Jamaican deejay culture is all about. He's apparently ridiculous: as an albino he has succeeded against odds most people couldn't begin to come to grips with; makes far more sense to his own crowd than he ever will to the outside world; truly understands the value of performance; and has a reservoir of self-belief you could turn a battleship round in. He opened the floodgates for deejays, because if this 'dundus' (as albinos are derogatively called in Jamaica) could have a go, and be so good at it, surely so could anybody. King Yellow was never less than spectacular, and 20 years ago ushered in an era that is, technically, stronger than it ever was – American mainstream interest is starting to pick up – but in actual fact climaxed with Shabba Ranks in the early 1990s.

Shabba in his pomp remains the high watermark of Jamaican deejaying – his entrance at a Sunsplash show, choppered in, at dawn, in his big sunglasses, satin click suit and wedgie haircut, to be handed a mic as he strode onstage with the crowd going crazy, summed up *everything* any deejay ought to be aiming for. True, Yellowman was always spectacular, Eek-A-Mouse made you laugh, Michigan & Smiley had the moves, but Shabba was the consummate showman. The effort Shabba put into what he did and how spectacularly it succeeded, gave deejaying a bona fideness that laid to rest the criticisms that still persist – that it's somehow inferior to singing because it's just some bloke talking and we could all do that. Couldn't we?

Shabba was one of the first seriously to try to crack America and his attitude was entirely right for it – he knew he had to compete with the rappers, was well aware of how much hard work went into their careers and seemed willing to take them on on their own terms. There's little doubt that, had he been handled better and America slightly more ready for him, there are very few rap acts Shabba Ranks couldn't have left choking in his dust when it came to holding a stage. It's doubly a shame he's not the force he once was, as in this American context the likes of Elephant Man,

Shabba Ranks

Bounty Killer, Lady Saw, Beenie Man and T.O.K. are the ones to watch, but it's a situation that would have fitted Shabba Ranks like one of his custom-made stage outfits. As the US becomes increasingly entertained by dancehall deejays, so video culture is becoming an enormous part of what they do and so the deejays' sense of style and scope to show off is getting even more spectacular. But whereas it was feared that over-involvement from MTV could have a detrimental, colonising-type effect on the finished product, deejays today seem to be rejecting any Americanisms and redefining dancehall style to almost surreal proportions within a very Jamaican set of parameters. Shabba should be part of this, as it's unlikely we've seen the half of what can be done.

Dennis Alcapone Describes the Art of Deejaying

What is toasting?

'Toasting is really to hype a record more, to get the crowd going in the dancehall and to really add something to music playing on the sound system. In the beginning, the deejay would be boosting up the sound system, bigging it up by singing its praises on the mic – it's the greatest, the best, with the best music, the most girls and so on – like he was toasting its success, that where the word comes from. It's the deejay who is on the mic, like a radio deejay, doing the talking, the guy who actually plays the records is the selector, because he selects the tunes.

'Whenever there would be a singer's record on in the dancehall, a vocal, the deejay would jive in between the singing, kind of answering what is being sung. Or after the vocal we'd play an instrumental version and the deejay would step up the pace by jiving the music – jive-talking over the top of it. This was to step up the pace in the dance, get the crowd in a frenzy because they love it when the deejay comes on because he's unique to their sound system.'

This was just live, on sound systems; when did deejays start recording?

'At the very end of the 1960s, when people like Duke Reid, who had a sound system and made records, realised quite how popular deejay record would be.'

And were they?

'Yes. Most certainly. At one time, back then, all the top positions in the Jamaican chart were held by deejay records and there was talk of them being banned from the chart. And it wasn't like there was a big flood of deejays, it was limited in those days to about four or five top deejays – U-Roy, Scotty, Lizzy Alcapone, Big Youth, myself and I-Roy.

'U-Roy was the originator of all modern deejay style, he actually turned the music that people was listening to in Jamaica into a new kind of music. In the beginning, some people didn't understand it because they were saying all we was doing was talking. Producers and all used to underrate it back then as well, but they wanted us to do it because it was selling. They'd say, "Come into the studio and voice this song", and probably you ain't got no lyrics for the song, but they didn't care, they just wanted to hear your voice because at the time it was selling. You would say to them, "Okay, first let me write some lyrics for that song and do it properly", and they'd say, "No man, just leave it, it'll be alright, we just want to hear you on the record and that's it". I've done some songs in my time that I'm not really proud of, but the producers didn't care as long as they had Dennis Alcapone's voice on the radio. That was all that mattered!

'They just wanted a vibe, and because there was a lot of money in this or the producers, and, as an artist to accumulate money you go to work for more than one producer, we'd be here, there and everywhere recording. Sometimes you'd have six tunes released in the week with six different producers.'

What was deejaying like before U-Roy?

'Before him, all deejays did was introduce records, "The spotlight now shines on a brother called Dennis Brown", like that, or they'd big up the sound system and announce a dance – you know: "This coming Saturday night, the great Sir George will be at such and such place, so make it a date and don't be late, it's gonna be great." That kind of thing was the deejay's job, so there wouldn't be a lot of lyrics going through the records being played, and not much that any producer could've put on a record.'

How did he change this?

'What U-Roy did was more or less what the singers were doing, just deejay style. He filled out the rhythm completely, so that it was a song, people could sing along, feel involved, because in the dancehall, Jamaican crowds wanted to feel part of what was happening, not just bystanders. He would work in between the singers, singers like The Melodians or The Paragons, the spaces where the singers aren't singing. He would kind of answer them, get involved in the song. Which is the same thing I and other deejays that came next came to do and we feel much better doing that, working with the singer, vibing off the song in between the lines, filling in the spaces.'

How did the producers react to this? Did they treat deejaying with any more respect?

'To be honest, at the time there was no way they think this thing was going to last. It was a just a one-off thing as far as they were concerned; it was a craze and like all crazes it would die down and not stand the test of time. That's why they didn't take it seriously. But the people love it and it's here now in the year 2002, it never die down. It's an art, a beautiful art and everybody accept it as such.'

The New Wave Of Roots Deejays

At the beginning of the 1970s, almost as soon as the generation of deejays led by U-Roy, Scotty, I-Roy and Dennis Alcapone had established the notion of deejays branching out of the dancehall and into the studios, they were usurped by a next wave that had more than scatting on their minds. Deejays like Big Youth, Prince Jazzbo, Trinity and Jah Stitch may have learned their techniques from checking out their predecessors at sound systems, but they were determined to take it a bit further stylistically and use it to communicate their dissatisfaction with life in general to their peers. It was the deejays who became the advance guard for roots'n'culture because of their empathy and swift exchange of ideas and opinions with their audience.

As Big Youth says: 'We wanted to teach the people, to educate them to what was going on around them. We wanted to put them in touch with each other and with Rasta, we knew what we had was too important just for "chick a bow".' Deejay style became important now, it wasn't enough just to imitate U-Roy: Big Youth's very musical style, Jazzbo's gravely tones, Trinity's story telling and so on got them noticed and set new benchmarks for what could be achieved.

Circumstances did a lot to give this generation a start, too. The Jamaican music business was beginning to fragment, as a combination of new technology and greater popular interest was bringing in a set of producers who were able to operate outside of the previous establishment.

Gussie Clarke, Keith Hudson and Niney the Observer were independents who appreciated the new styles and sentiments of these deejays and were able to record them. They were addressing an audience much the same age as they were, and therefore understood perfectly what was required. Gussie Clarke sums up this deejay revolution as he tells the story of *Screaming Target*, the album he produced for Big Youth.

'It was the second recording I actually did, and I knew Big Youth because we lived in the same area. I wouldn't have said either of us recognised a new wave coming, but we were young – I was barely out of high school – and hungry to produce records, to get involved. I was never a follower and was looking for different ideas, and *Screaming Target* evolved over the period of time that we were making it rather than from a set of preconceived ideas. We used a lot of effects on Big Youth's vocals, because they were available and we wanted to see how far we could go with them. We knew what was happening around us was kind of staid, so we wanted to put more excitement into it, the other young producers thought that way too, and there was a sense of competition among us. Then, of course there was Big Youth, a new kid on the block, so he's prepared to take more chances and a great artist already, but still with a lot of potential. But the main thing was to do something different.'

Big Youth

Beenie Man

Beenie Man

There is a special relationship between Jamaican sound system deejays and their audiences, even if this sometimes doesn't extend to their immediate family. As illustrated by Beenie Man's entry into the field.

'I started in the deejay business from the day I was born! From the day I knew myself start talking, I started singing, because as a kid I had a bad stammer and couldn't talk straight, unless I sung like a deejay. I had to sing to get the words out straight. I would read a book, I would sing the words and so on. So it seemed natural to start to do it professionally, and my uncle had a sound system in the community where I'm from, Master Blaster International, and he take me along.

'I was five years old, and being a kid in the dancehall, I've got lots of love from the people, because they haven't seen a kid my age holding the mic and doing it professionally. It wasn't a nursery rhyme thing either, it was proper lyrics. Because of my size, I have to go on boxes, so people can really see who I am, but they love it. The people really appreciate me and the applause was great, greater than even anybody else who was there. They treat me as theirs straight away, and it give me the courage and the encouragement to pursue a career.

'That's the first time I get a proper beating from my mother too, because I'd dodged out of the house when everybody was sleeping. I just leave out to go to the dance because I know this was my break, and although I get a beating, I know that I will sleep and when I wake up the whole community will respect me. And that's how I start.'

Eighties deejays, left to right: Roger Steppers; General Trees; Flourgon; Burru Banton

8
dub crazy

Niney 'The Observer' Holness

With the exception, of course, of a sizeable proportion of tourists, in Jamaica nothing gets wasted. It's very much a part of the Jamaican psyche, that you need to be inventive with whatever is put in front you. Why throw a tune away just because it's been a hit?

Back in the late 1960s, when dub and version first got noticed as a significant part of reggae's release schedule, it baffled outside observers, that the same tune would get done over several times. Such behaviour was generally sneered at as a sign of creative bankruptcy or sheer bone-idleness, and the idea that the instrumental version, the dub version and the (several) toasting versions could each be released as a new record was assumed to be some sort of con trick. Its acceptance, however, in Jamaica, isn't at all surprising. There's always been a cover-version culture in the island's music, which has resulted in people not being too bothered about having heard a tune before or taking it more seriously because it's already proven. Many older people blame this on a Colonial-induced national inferiority complex that tends to rate imports far above their homegrown equiva-lent. But there's far more to it than that. The fact that copyright laws weren't applied to music until a few years ago contributed too, because if you

wanted to do over somebody else's song you didn't have to worry about clearances. Importantly though, if a song or a backing track has dominated the Jamaican sound systems and airwaves for a month or so it doesn't mean people will be fed up. Exactly the opposite, in fact. It proves how much they like it, making it ideal for retreading. And as for the notion of creative laziness, some of the effort that goes into reworking a tune is far greater than what went into making the original. Men like King Tubby, Errol T, Scientist and Mikey Dread are among the music's biggest stars – Tubby is an acknowledged genius – yet what they do is remix other people's work.

Over the past 30-odd years, dubbing or versioning has become an artform in its own right and one of reggae's most unique and instantly identifiable strands. It's an inspired and inspiring world where every rhythm track has an open-ended shelf life and every song can stand at least

King Tubby

one more take on it. A world where it's not unusual to find entire albums devoted to singularly different approaches to a single backing track, where drum and bass parts resurface two decades after they first hit big and the studio becomes an instrument in its own right, with whoever's operating the mixing desk as the most important player. Without dub, it's safe to say there would be no Fatboy Slim, hardly any Massive Attack and a great big hole in dance music where its remix culture ought to be. And to think, all this happened by accident.

The story is that, in 1967, a sound system operator called Ruddy Redwood was given a dubplate of The Paragons' 'On The Beach', but his disc cutter had literally forgotten to put the vocal on. Intrigued by the notion of an instrumental cut of a proven crowd-pleaser, Redwood dropped this new version immediately after he'd spun the vocal. Within seconds, he knew he'd stumbled on something significant as the crowd took up the song and sung it themselves all the way through. In celebration, he put this new version on again … and again … and again. Naturally, it didn't take long for news of this success to spread and everybody to start wanting versions. Quite apart from allowing a sound system operator to extend the natural life of one of his key tunes, it also provided space for a deejay to toast the sound without fighting against a vocal. To build on this interaction, the more proficient disc cutters could drop the vocals in and out of a dub plate, allowing for a musical joust between the original singers and the deejays, thus cranking up the excitement levels a few more notches.

Among the *most* proficient of these disc cutters was the legendary King Tubby, the man who went from simply making holes in the mix for deejays to do their thing, to fading the voices and instruments in and out of the final mix with such imagination and precision he spun new tunes out of old. King Tubby turned the mixing desk into the most important aspect of any recording, he would play it accordingly, and as an electronics wizard, his mixing desk was no ordinary piece of kit. He started off with a number of homemade frequency filters that would be used to cut out the different instruments and then drop them back in. When he got a proper mixing desk he immediately made some modifications and would rebuild circuits every time he couldn't achieve an effect he wanted. His outboard equipment, like echo machines, sound-effects packages and cross faders, were either self-built or customised out of all recognition. And, as technology moved on, he was usually one step in front of it, acquiring and then altering anything new that came on the market. All in a spare room in his mum's house too. Pretty soon, Tubby had a queue of Jamaica's top producers wanting him to remix most of their output and a fair amount of their back catalogue. A perfect arrangement: they owned the tunes so why not recycle them? Apart from paying the remixer it was pure profit and dancehall patrons weren't complaining as these days soundmen competed by playing the freshest version of an old favourite.

Following in the great man's slipstream were any number of engineers and producers trying to

achieve similar results. As technology advanced, their lives were made considerably easier and it took off to the point that, during the 1970s, one of the features of roots reggae was the dread-style remixes that would transport the most innocuous love songs into their own portentous nyahbingi. Soon it went wider than that and, via disco, remixing crossed into the world at large, but it shouldn't be forgotten that it all leads back to King Tubby. In Jamaica, this is a relatively straightforward route because if you trace a line through reggae's most innovative remixers it'll quickly end up at Tubby's door: King Jammy worked for Tubby as an engineer, as did Scientist; Bobby Digital worked for Jammy's; Mikey Dread was a protégé and close friend of Tubby …

As dancehall took over from roots at the end of the 1970s, the whole notion of recycling rhythms was taken to another level. Rather than rework a tune in a dub fashion as had been the case, if a producer built a rhythm that proved popular they'd version it by putting as many different deejays or singers on it – separately, of course – as the market would bear. As might be expected, this practice had its origins in the dancehall, where soundmen would attempt to top each other not by spinning an exclusive tune, but by dropping an exclusive vocal take of the record their opponent had just played. Which, when you think about it, is actually more of a diss. Thus, sound system specials became all about getting new and distinctive deejays to ride a well-worn rhythm.

This is how the dancehall trend for sustaining rhythms came into being. It was simply sound system-savvy record producers duplicating what was going on at the dance by releasing newer and newer deejay cuts of the same rhythm – 'Boops', 'Punany', 'Sleng Teng', 'Stalag 17', 'Playground' … are just some of the rhythms that have had hundreds of versions released. Although few producers will actually admit it, it will be at the back of their minds when building a rhythm that it ought to be such that it could support an inordinate amount of retreads without the public getting bored with it.

Whether this way of working is now short-circuiting creativity is genuinely open to question. In its current approach to music, it doesn't seem to be stretching too many people too far, and it can't be unconnected to the fact that little new talent is coming through and the same deejays have been dominating the scene for the past 10 years. It's creating an apparently unhealthy imbalance between artists and producers too. These days, the producer/studio owner selects a rhythm, and then he curtly calls in one of the young hopeful deejays idling in his yard waiting for a break and gets him to voice it with his own lyrics. Then pays him a fixed sum. At a time when much of Jamaica's music business seems to be taking care of its business properly, this harks back to the near feudalism of the ska and rock steady days, and will not be doing a great deal for artist or musical development.

While this way of doing things, is so entrenched, it's difficult to see how it's going to change, but this is the Jamaican music business, where nothing stays the same for too long.

King Jammy's Remembers King Tubby's

King Jammy aka Lloyd James is one of modern reggae's most successful producers. And so he should be, he apprenticed under the great King Tubby. Here he looks back at his late mentor.

'King Tubby's have a style that nobody else have, so producers used to cling to him, but apart from his style, his mixing console had certain features that other didn't have. He had a high-pass filter built into the console with a slide, so when he was mixing a dub, he could swing the frequency from a low frequency to high and keep on swaying it. For his echo he used to use another four-track tape machine patched into the board so he always used a tape echo and could gauge it to any speed he wanted.

'I couldn't say if he invented dub or not, but surely he was the dub master, he was the best of the time. I would say he was a genius, a self-taught genius. The way he approached a tune was a strictly spur-of-the-moment thing, he didn't just go into the studio and sit there all day, he used to sit in his office, cooling off and having a conversation, then, when the vibes or the situation was right, he'd just go in and start mixing. He didn't rehearse or anything, and he was a master of his equipment, so he could work like this.

'He was a very neat man – neat and complete. He was a perfectionist, you couldn't do no second thing for him, you had to come with the best for him to accept it, because he would never stop trying until he get it the right way. But he was a very nice guy to be around, very helpful, very encouraging. He used to sit there all day or all night with singers trying to make a song, he'd give them lyrics or encourage them to take it further. He had a genuine love for music and didn't know anything other than electronics and music, but he know them so well.

'He was a humble man, stayed humble throughout. He wasn't seeking praise for what he'd done, even with an album like *King Tubbys Meets Rockers Uptown* he was just doing things because he was doing them, it wouldn't affect him how big anything got. He's always talk about doing things different from other people, and that was really what he wanted to achieve. He had a good sense of humour though. You can hear it in his mixes, they're full of humour, and that was one of the things that gave him the advantage over other mixers. He always crack off a joke in the studio too, we used to laugh things off … always. In those days, we just used to enjoy ourselves doing the music, it was different from now.'

King Tubbys Meets Rockers Uptown

'Tubby used to work with a lot of producers, but Augustus Pablo was one of his favourites, like a special producer friend, because he started there when Tubby's was just about to open his studio, so they went back a long way. Not everybody was allowed to smoke herb in Tubby's studio, but Pablo was special, so he do his thing with his pipe anywhere! So Pablo used to get special preferential treatment and Tubby would put his heart and soul into anything Pablo brought him, so I know he gave that album a little bit extra to make it successful.'

Left: Keith Hudson back in the day

Below: Tubby used to work with a lot of producers, but Augustus Pablo was one of his favourites

King Jammy's at the controls

9
great britain

Brinsley from Aswad

British reggae is often talked about as a contradiction in terms, like British rap: it can't exist in any form that even comes close to credibility, and if it doesn't come from Jamaica – or maybe specifically Kingston – it just doesn't count. British reggae is not and never will be the genuine article.

It's astonishing how many people actually believe and actively promote the above diatribe. And these aren't characters who have as their UK reggae role models 10cc and The Police. Traditionally, British reggae's harshest critics are those that have immersed themselves in what's made in Jamaica, even if they were born and bred in Blighty themselves. Confusing really, given that what's been going on in Reggae Britannia – that is, in the netherworld of sound systems, clubs, small labels and specialist shops, far away from the aforementioned pop fodder – has usually been inventive, open-minded and always relative to its environment. In other words, it's been built along essentially Jamaican guidelines, but very often has ended up being labelled as some sort of idiot cousin that it's best not to talk about.

Of course, it's only comparatively recently that there was any British reggae. In the very early days of ska, Jamaican music was imported into this country with exactly the sort of informality you'd expect –

people with music business connections back home would run sound systems and flog records door-to-door. There had been, since the 1950s, a vibrant scene of small clubs, dances and house parties that supported sound systems like Duke Vin's and Count Suckle's, and when records started selling in JA those same tunes would be bought in England as souvenirs of home, but interest in Jamaican music didn't extend much beyond the Jamaican immigrant community. True, the mods adopted Prince Buster and took on ska as part of their amphetamine-fuelled black music soundtrack, but it wasn't until the enormous success of 'My Boy Lollipop' in 1964, a record made in London and specifically aimed at the mainstream UK market, that any sort of wider audience was proven to exist.

By the late 1960s, after several years of healthy underground sales to, mainly, the white working classes, the British pop world on the whole discovered reggae. It was scorned by the media, especially by the BBC, most of whose on-air representatives were quite open in their contempt. But, in spite of such open hostility to all reggae, Desmond Dekker, Nicky Thomas, Bob & Marcia *et al* complemented The Jackson Five, The Supremes and Chairman Of The Board in the UK charts and dancehalls. Reggae sold by the lorry load, and Jamaican record producers reacted to what became the biggest single market in the world for their product by making music specifically tailored for it: rhythm tracks were sent over to be embellished with orchestral arrangements (it was the only way the BBC would play reggae records); lyrics were hastily penned to include UK-friendly references; and the tempo was shifted up a gear to make allowances for the cold weather (honestly!). As Britain moved into the 1970s, there was a new breed of black youngsters coming of age: the children of the first wave of immigrants or those that had arrived in the UK very young. These guys were, to all intents and purposes, British, but the majority in their host nation refused to see it this way. They had been educated to both British standards (which were actually pretty good then) and expectations, but were now having great difficulty pursuing their chosen careers as institutional racism was ubiquitous. The police were on their backs every time they left their houses, and they could forget driving a car in a built-up area. And their parents were largely unsympathetic.

It meant there was a statelessness that was as cultural as it was literal, as nothing that existed in Britain or, up that point, Jamaica seemed to address their issues. Black American soul music came close but it still didn't quite do the job. Roots reggae, however, was a perfect fit. Naturally, these young guys wanted to contribute to their own music, and, just as naturally, they were going to bring the influences that were all around them – pop, soul, rock and so on – to what they did. This really was the first generation of British reggae: just because the pleasant pop-chart fodder of before sold well in Britain and some of it was made there, it was never really *British*, it didn't really *connect* in the way the homegrown roots generation of Matumbi, Steel Pulse, Aswad, Misty In Roots, Black Slate, Delroy Washington and Reggae Regular did. They sang about the situation in England in an accent that was as discernibly London or Birmingham as it was Jamaican and did it in a band situation that pushed the approach to the music forward. Impeccable reggae credentials – it acknowledged its environment, borrowed shamelessly from the outside world and was constantly looking to evolve.

Maybe it was because so many of these players weren't of Jamaican descent (Dennis Bovell, for instance, is Barbadian and Aswad's Brinsley Forde is Guyanese), or perhaps because they'd spent their formative years in the UK, but theirs was a reggae that removed itself from the often assumed tyranny of Kingston. It didn't labour under the obsessive necessity of behaving as 'Jamaican' as possible, and so could open up the music in all manner of different directions. Then, because they fully understood the music they were dealing with, they never swerved from what it was supposed to do; in other words, no matter how clever they got, they didn't neglect the rhythm section. It's hard to imagine such intricate, progressive reggae records as 'Handsworth Revolution', 'Rock' or 'Warrior Charge' being made anywhere other than England. The local sound systems loved them, they went down a storm in Jamaica too, yet they seemed to put so many critics' backs up at the time. Still do, remarkably, although even with hindsight it's got no less difficult to see why.

It was the same for the wave that came next, Smiley Culture, Asher Senator, Maxi Priest, Tippa Irie and the like, with their pop-orientated dancehall lite. All those guys had top-notch sound system credentials, as they'd come up through the ranks, but they'd opted to make a bit of a mainstream splash and had brought all their experience to bear on what appeared to be throwaway pop ditties. They, too, took all manner of media stick for having little more than novelty value. It doesn't really matter whether you'd actually listen to 'Police Officer' or 'Hello Darling' out of choice, the point is that those records had to have serious reggae skills involved in them in order to come across that casual without falling flat.

Back in the 1970s though, there was another facet of British reggae that was easily as important as its roots developments, a music that sold in phenomenal quantities, and although seldom in chart return shops, it did hit the mainstream Top Twenty on several memorable occasions. It was lovers rock, the frothy, girlie side of things, which was deliberately devised as the flip-side of roots to satisfy the less rebellious, more conventional romantics among Britain's new black population. It was the first real British black pop music, and went as far as to influence the music back in Jamaica.

Its stars were teenagers like Janet Kay, Carroll Thompson, Brown Sugar, Ginger Williams and Louisa Mark, with the boys represented by Trevor Walters, Victor Romero Evans and Peter Hunningale, who were essentially no different from their audience – aspirational, smart and hopelessly in love. The songs told photo-story romance tales of love, love lost and love looked for, accompanied by booming reggae beats that were made lighter by the attention to melody and upper-register harmonising.

Lovers rock proved so popular that Jamaican reggae stars would come over, immerse themselves in the style and then record in that fashion after returning to Jamaica, where their releases found a similar level of support as they did in the UK. Dennis Brown, Gregory Isaacs and Johnny Osbourne all owe a great deal to what was going on in London at the time.

It's hardly surprising, then, that British reggae more or less gave up some time in the 1980s, but whereas it might have vanished as a music, it has remained in the mix as an attitude and an influence. Soul II Soul, internationally the most successful black British group so far, freely admit to owing their whole way of doing things to their life as the North London reggae sound system Jah Rico. Jungle, the underground black pop style, has a reggae basis to it and its one big hit, 'Incredible', was by General Levy, a respected London sound system deejay. Then there's So Solid Crew, UK garage's highest profile exponents, who will laugh when you ask them about their reggae influences because, to them, the British take on Jamaican music that they all grew up with is so intrinsic a part of what they do that it doesn't even bear thinking about.

Not bad for something that has been written off for the best part of 30 years.

Left: Caron Wheeler, a lover's rock star with Brown Sugar *and* the voice of Soul II Soul

Right: Jazzy B and Daddae, brought reggae methods to Soul II Soul

Below: Aswad, the Lions of Ladbroke Grove, still in the cubs

David Hinds

As a member of Steel Pulse, David Hinds was an integral part of the British-made roots music scene in the 1970s, when acts like Black Slate, Matumbi, Aswad and Misty In Roots favoured a group situation.

'The black youth of my generation got affiliated to reggae music through our parents. They came over to England in the 1950s; many of us had brothers and sisters in Jamaica and as our parents could afford to bring them over one by one they'd come, bringing with them the latest craze of music, the latest dance that came with it and whatever political statements or political climate that was happening in Jamaica at the time. So we'd take on board that this was more than just a music, and as we started to grow up we gravitated to the music even more because we were learning about ourselves through it.

'There was a serious identity crisis happening in Handsworth, where we were from, and in various black communities throughout England at the time. Our parents' ideologies stem from a lot of Victorian standards, which came from their

Steel Pulse

parents, who were born at the turn of the century, because that was the way it was in Jamaica. Our parents were running away from Jamaica, trying to start a new life in England, but still adhered to a lot of the old-fashioned ways that were taught to them by their parents. But we're in a new country where there was a new approach to life as far as we were concerned – many of us had never had that Jamaican experience – so there were a lot of clashes as far as what was considered best for us.

'We needed to learn about ourselves as black people, and we definitely weren't learning it at school, but we found what we were looking for in the music. We played a lot of Bob Marley songs, The Abyssinians, Burning Spear … a lot of Burning Spear because he uttered the words of Marcus Garvey and a lot of educational stuff. As a result, we got ourselves together and thought it was necessary to air our views through the music.

'We had a lot to say too, because as we found ourselves as people, we felt it was important to document what was happening to us. As we got older in Handsworth there was always this racial thing hovering over our heads and we had to be always on our guard when we go on the streets. The police was always giving trouble, then we found a lot of problems having jobs although we'd had the education. It was an uphill struggle, but we couldn't explain to our parents what we were about living in England, so to do it in music was our best outlet.

'Our track "Ku Klux Klan", that particular subject was in the papers at the time, as there was talk about the Grand Wizard coming over here to influence the head of the National Front. My imagination just got the better of me and I started imagining white extremists on the streets of Handsworth. The title track of the album *Handsworth Revolution* was because of the political climate in England, especially in the black communities, and with the first riot taking place in St Pauls in Bristol it was only a matter of time before all the black communities would be going up in flames. "Blues Dance Raid" was about having house parties in our own community because we weren't made to feel welcome in the city centre, so this was the only chance the West Indian community had to rave. But neighbours would be calling the police saying the music is too loud or we got some scary-looking people walking on the streets … whatever reasons. Then the police would come and try to close the place down and they didn't particularly care how they did it. And it was important for us to call the album *Handsworth Revolution* because UK reggae always comes from a London perspective and they think in Birmingham we were known as country bumpkins.

'Because this was our best way of expressing how we felt about what we were going through – the way we could get most people to listen – all the English reggae bands had plenty to say at the time. Aswad with "Three Babylon", "Not Satisfied", "Back To Africa"; Matumbi with "Rock", "Guide Us" or "Music In The Air"; Black Slate with "Sticks Man"; Misty In Roots … Pablo Gad … Reggae Regular's "Where Is Jah"? … the UK roots bands all had plenty to say for themselves.'

Babylon's Victor Romero Evans and Brinsley Forde

Franco Rosso's movie *Babylon* presented such an accurate snapshot of young black life in London at the beginning of the 1980s, it achieved instant cult status and has yet to be bettered. Brinsley Forde of Aswad and lovers rock icon Victor Romero Evans starred in it.

Victor: 'There hadn't been a lot of films depicting black life in England, especially young black life. At that time there was a big surge in black theatre, plays about young people, but no films, so *Babylon* meant we were moving in the right direction. This was something that was going to show a piece of our lives on a big scale, it meant we were being taken seriously, so it meant a lot in that sense. There was one other, *Burning An Illusion*, but this seemed like a bigger project and it had this street element which I hadn't seen depicted before. It looked like we were going to move forward from there. My big regret is that there hasn't really been anything since – in twenty years – and I don't know if that's our fault as we black people ought to be producing our own material. Hopefully, we'll put that right.'

Brinsley: '*Babylon* opened a lot of people's eyes to what was actually going on around them as stuff like that had never been on the big screen before. Even some of the actors that were in it learned from it. We had this scene depicting the youth standing up for themselves and facing down the police, and Karl Howman, one of the actors, found that very distressing and insisted that this wouldn't happen in London. For a white person in early 82 he just didn't understand that those things happened in England – we had to bring in news film to show him police coming in with dogs breaking up crowds of youths and then he began to understand.

'After the riots in London, Lord Scarman asked to see *Babylon*, because it was very, very close to the mark of what was happening in London and the political problems and social problems that were happening in England.'

Lover's Rock

While UK roots reggae may have had a high mainstream media profile, it wasn't the only strictly British aspect of reggae that was capturing the imaginations, and purchasing power, of a new generation of 'born here' black youngsters. Big in the blues dances and specialist record shops of the 1970s and early 1980s was lovers rock, the flip side to roots reggae, aimed at a more upmarket, aspirational young black crowd and unique to the UK inasmuch as it couldn't have happened anywhere else and ended up being exported back to Jamaica.

Janet Kay and Carroll Thompson are two of the acknowledged queens of lovers rock, and here they remember how important it was to that particular generation.

What was lovers rock?

Janet: 'It was the music I wanted to make to express the kind of reggae and the kind of music that I listened to. I was into a lot of Motown, pop, Beatles and such like, from the age of five or six, I used to idolise people like Lulu and Dusty Springfield because that was what I saw on TV, the Beatles was what I heard on the radio and I'd buy all the Motown records because they were the black singers at the time. So when I got to do reggae music I wanted to put something else into it, that Motown influence, the soul influence … Deniece Williams … Candi Staton … '

Carroll: 'Lovers rock was just having good love songs, nice arrangements, pretty vocals and pretty background vocals. I'd grown up with all that stuff Janet did, Motown, Michael Jackson, Minnie Riperton, Earth, Wind & Fire … and then all the pop stuff from the UK as well. We were absorbing all those pop sensibilities and not really knowing, so it was natural that it should all come out in our reggae music.'

How was it regarded by the reggae world?

Carroll: 'It was like a lukewarm version of reggae – some thrown-away child that nobody really wanted!'

Who was it aimed at?

Carroll:'We weren't thinking about it on a marketing level at all. I think the producers knew that women or young girls were into this music because they weren't into roots and culture so much. We had a passion for music and we gravitated towards this as something that best expressed who we were and what our lives were. It was something that felt completely natural for us.'

Janet: 'There were a lot more girls out there like us, and it did give other girls something to latch on to that wasn't there before. But we didn't really realise they were here when we started out.'

Carroll: 'It was this audience that, like us, didn't really feel part of the Fari movement. I just couldn't go out there singing about roots and culture and back to Africa because I didn't feel it represented me. I understood what it was about, but I didn't feel I could do the Judy Mowatt thing and go out there and dress up in robes and do that.

Janet: 'It wasn't something you thought about, it was something you did. We were like the second generation black people here so we didn't have anything to follow, we could do what came naturally.'

Carroll: 'It was the youth of that generation expressing themselves the only way they knew how. That's why there was such a musical explosion. And the big thing about lovers rock was there was never much difference between the fans and the performers.'

It used to be said that it ignored the plight of black people in Britain, was that true?

Janet: 'Well, there was "Black Pride" by Brown Sugar and there were other conscious lovers songs, but so often it got dismissed because we were female and the whole thing was too light.'

Carroll: 'Lyrically, "Black Pride" says black is the colour of my skin, black is the life that I live, I'm so proud to be the colour God made me … I think it did sum a lot of things up. We had things like the Brixton riots, the New Cross fire, you had so many things happening, the SUS laws, things happening at the Carnival, things happening politically, and, of course, we were aware of all that. That song and others showed how we felt, but I guess we

Janet Kay

were always overshadowed in that area by the Aswads and Steel Pulses and everyone else coming up with a very militant steppers thing and we were just women singing beautifully.'

10
raggamuffin time

Eek-A-Mouse

My personal favourite reason for how dancehall reggae got its name is that it was reggae the radio wouldn't play, therefore its sole outlet was the sound systems in the dancehalls. It almost excuses the gun talk and slackness, implying they were deliberately designed to enhance any outlaw status.

The problem is, this isn't entirely an accurate description. Dancehall reggae got its name because of where it came from rather than where it *wasn't* going, and in spite of the romanticism of the above notion, the music had to exist for the radio to reject it. What dancehall reggae is, however, and this in itself endorses the rebel spirit of the island's music community, is one of the most vivid examples of how reggae's cyclical nature works to keep it sharp and strong.

Modern Jamaican music is people's music. It has been since ska usurped American R&B, and it has remained that way to such a degree it's probably the last, still-evolving, genuine folk music – or at least it's the one with the highest profile. It has stayed that way because it has never moved too far from those same Jamaican people. Literally, as well as figuratively. Go to a sound system dance or a concert performance and it's hard to work out just by looking who's a performer and who's a punter. Then, once those same stars go off duty,

they'll be back among the general population, often in the area they grew up. It's this sense of artists and audience belonging to each other, and being well aware of such mutual ownership, that is unique to Jamaica. Maybe that's because it's an island. However, if this closeness starts to get stretched, that is, if the music goes wide and outside forces start to exert too great an influence, it pulls itself back to Kingston's inner city communities to re-emerge in a form that makes little or no immediate sense to the outside world. A kind of re-establishing of proprietorship. It happened when ska changed into rock steady, just after it went uptown; or when happy, shiny reggae earned itself an international following in the late-1960s, roots'n'culture rumbled out of the ghetto. The emergence of dancehall reggae at the top of the following cycle took this whole notion of self-preservation through the roof, to such a degree that for the first time in its 40-year history, it's now possible for reggae as a music to move into the mainstream without essential compromise.

Buju Banton

Immediately prior to dancehall, roots reggae's success had been remarkable. Way beyond merely Marley, the likes of Third World, Black Uhuru, Culture and Burning Spear had become internationally acknowledged, signed to major record companies and made albums for world consumption, and as a result their priorities and considerations were becoming far less parochial. It was as if roots reggae didn't really belong to the home crowd any longer, and therefore was becoming increasingly less relevant. This state of affairs was exacerbated by a political sea change – in 1980, Michael Manley's roots-encouraging PNP was ousted by the right-wing, free-enterprisish JLP; then there was a general feeling among the sufferah classes that 10 years of beating down Babylon hadn't achieved an awful lot. The time had come to dance to a different beat, one controlled from downtown and far more proletariat hands-on than reggae had become. Of course, this was going to come to pass on the sound systems.

This being Jamaica, the obvious place to start moving forward was in the past, so as a way of finding something new, the sound system operators began dusting off classic Studio One and rock steady rhythms. And the best way to freshen these tracks up was to have a bang-up-to-the-minute, new-generation deejay toasting over the top. These were local guys, young guys who had their own styles and lyrical ideas, who had probably never been near a recording studio and were performing solely for the appreciation and enjoyment of their own crowd. Such a situation took reggae right back to its own basics; both the performers and the crowds responded to each other, encouraging a new type of music to evolve as an almost wholly communal development.

Effectively removed from any greater commercial pressure than simply rocking the house – which, don't get me wrong, could be far more personally stressful than chart placings – dancehall took its own course. Naturally, there was going to be a rush of deejays as more or less anybody could pick up the mic at the dance, or at least they could pick it up *once*, but it wasn't without its singers. And this was a generation far more concerned with pleasures of the flesh than praising Jah Jah. Why bother with sufferation when you could nice up the dance? It created a situation where the art of deejaying took a step back to the halcyon days of Daddy U-Roy, King Stitt and Dennis Alcapone when it was all about urging the dancers on, bigging up the sound system, commenting on the dancehall soap opera unfolding around them or bouncing off the record itself. Most significantly though, in these expressions of sheer celebration, scatting was coming back in a big way. 'Bim', 'ribbit', 'hey-ah', 'oink' and 'eee-haw' were all entirely acceptable as a part of early dancehall's lyrical flow.

Indeed, this jive talking neatly sums up this particular period, as after a decade or so of the sort of piousness and strength of purpose involved in roots reggae, many wanted just to mess about. Reggae got its sense of humour back. A knockabout, cartoon-fashion sense of fun as deejays such as Michigan & Smiley, Lone Ranger, Burru Banton and General Echo preceded the almost surreal likes of Eek-A-Mouse and Yellowman. Also, with the sheer number of deejays coming through at this time, and an apparently limited lyrical subject matter, scatting allowed deejays to make their own mark – every early 1980s deejay who made an impression had a signature noise or nonsense expression. Such carryings-on added enormously to the sense of competition among the deejays – another old-time aspect – and, most importantly, it worked hard to keep it ghetto-centric, as so much of what was going on or being said would have totally confused pop music's mainstream.

Beyond the scatting, a great deal of dancehall's content – misogyny, homophobia, gun glorification – has long given cause for concern, and quite rightly too. Its degeneration happened later, after the music had gone out into the wider world and begun to feel the sway of outside influences and opinions. At the time we're talking about here, there was an admittedly limited breadth of subject matter largely because the deejays and the crowds themselves had limited life experience. They chatted about what they knew and what they knew their audiences knew. Which, to a large degree, was sex. After all, what are most people in the dancehall for? To pull. And there's a tradition in Caribbean music that holds bawdiness in truly high esteem: calypso would have collapsed years ago without its staple diet of sex talk; and back in the late 1960s, rude reggae was so prevalent it became an accepted musical sub-genre.

It was this slackness – a highly entertaining, saucy, almost 'Carry On' approach to a lyric – that also did so much to define dancehall. It was

Capleton on London's White City Estate

diametrically opposed to roots'n'culture, relevant to its immediate environment and made stars of General Echo, Lone Ranger and, brightest of them all, Yellowman. The latter was an albino deejay with a phenomenal ability to improvise both musically

and narratively and a sense of panache that had him dubbed King Yellow by a downtown public that clearly still adore him. It was a crucial manifestation of dancehall's internalisation and Jamaican contrariness that the crowds should adopt as their spiritual leader an outcast – in Jamaica, albinos are shunned, as Yellowman was, by even their immediate family. Yet here he was singing about girls being crazy over him, and indeed they were. At one point in the early 1980s, when Yellowman came to London to do shows, his crowds stopped traffic. Yet he was hardly heard of, let alone

long there weren't any records. It existed solely in the dancehall, but with the sort of momentum that had been building up, it was only a matter of time before it did get onto vinyl, especially with the popularity of dancehall tapes convincing producers there was a market here. These were cassettes knocked off from the control tower at sound system sessions, rapidly duplicated and sold out of boxes at the dancehall or on the street. They were also beginning seriously to challenge the sales of more conventional recordings. It can't be a coincidence that the biggest names in early dancehall-style recordings were all sound system owners, therefore well aware of what was going on. Henry 'Junjo' Lawes, King Jammy and Bobby Digital owned, respectively, Volcano, King Jammy's Super Power and Heatwave and represented one more aspect of dancehall returning reggae to the traditions established 20 years previously by Coxsone, Prince Buster and Duke Reid.

Since those early, glorious days, dancehall reggae has become a lot of things, not all of them good, but what it did was put control of the music back in the hands of the people it was made by and for. With technological advances making high-quality recording more and more accessible, those same people have been able to remain in charge of it, twisting and turning it to suit themselves and thus making sure their true souls come out. Today, it's exactly that soul and not some marketing meeting's approximation of it, that big-time pop and rock acts like No Doubt are coming to Jamaica looking for. A bit like when The Stones, The Clash and Paul Simon came down in the 1970s.

appreciated by the mainstream reggae audiences that had been eagerly buying the roots albums. But we're getting ahead of ourselves.

To address the point made at the beginning of this chapter, the main reason dancehall reggae didn't get played on the radio was because for so

Above: Big Yellow still reigns supreme in down town Kingston

Left: Frankie Paul carried conventional singing and style into dancehall

Yellowman

Were you the first deejay to go wide with the slackness tunes?

'Not really, in those days there was General Echo with *The Slackest LP* in 1979, but people put the whole slackness thing on me because I expand on it more than Echo did in his career time. But I never really know what they call slackness … what I talk is not slackness, because what I talk is reality. Like if I say sex, I talk about sex. It's what happens behind closed door, but it happens. That is reality, but people call it slackness.'

Did you have to work hard at it?

'No, it just come natural. I don't really think about it, because I am a man and that's how man think about the girls.'

It worked with the girls, didn't it? Why was that?

'Because I'm a man, so girls will always come after a man. Because I look different too. But really, I think it's because I say the things that woman like, I use the words that guys love to hear about woman and woman love to hear about themselves. So they loved me. Even now they love me because what they love is a man who talk nice about them. Say they're pretty, they're beautiful, they're sexy, they're nice.'

Did you think the other deejays had been neglecting them?

'They never pay the girls enough attention, the deejay thing was about man too much. They used to talk about the stuff that please the guys like gun or ganja or something. Then, when they do talk about woman they don't talk nice things, they say the woman a bitch or a whore. Women don't want to hear that. They want to hear nice things, sexy things. That's the reason why the girls love me … because I love them.'

Sly & Robbie

Around the time dancehall was redefining reggae in one direction, Sly Dunbar and Robbie Shakespeare, the music's most dynamic rhythm section, were using the same computer technology to take it down another avenue. Their groundbreaking work with vocal trio Black Uhuru defined much of early 1980s reggae with a crisp, hard sound that was obviously computerised yet at the same time very human. They maintain that this is because they are musicians rather than technicians, so when they operate computers, they're still always looking for what's musical rather than simply what sounds exciting. But, as it turns out, that classic Black Uhuru sound wasn't even developed for that particular group.

Sly: 'Robbie and myself, we get the idea from touring with Peter Tosh. We knew that the one drop was good, but what we saw from that tour was it needed more energy. So when we get back we just started to experiment with sounds and went into it with a different attitude and start to discover that open snare thing …'

Robbie: 'It's a rock'n'roll thing, because on tour we were in more of that sort of environment …'

Sly and Robbie

Sly: '... yeah, a rock'n'roll thing because we mix that guitar in it on "Shine Eye Gal". This was a song that had much more energy, because with that snare sound it could lift and then come down, wham! You couldn't go any harder than this. It was the different attitude that got us there, because we were thinking about when you're in a stadium with fifty thousand people, the standard one drop will be so light you can't hear it, but if you open the snare and slap, it everybody hears it.

'Then, once we'd created this different kind of sound we play it in a sense that it's a groove and then when we get it going me and Robbie can play what we feel like playing inside it. But it's so strong that there's people who are not musical who can understand what we're doing. We play R&B within it, we play soul, we don't need to play straight reggae, that way we know it will sound different but would still, basically, be reggae.'

What Came First? The Rhythm or the Dance

As the dancehall era changed how reggae was approached, the way the music was made became similar to how it had been in the beginning. Moving away from the artist-centric 1970s, when there were more reggae bands than before and singers and musicians were writing their own songs and getting them made, as the 1980s progressed, producers increasingly called the shots, building rhythms and bringing in deejays (usually) to voice them. As a result, certain rhythms would be used over and over and over again with only the vocals changed, and the same tune would dominate reggae for months on end. These rhythms were named after the big initial hit and among those that had, literally, several hundred versions are 'Stalag 17', 'Punany' and 'Bogle'.

And another aspect harking back to a bygone era was the new dances inspired by these rhythms, or should that be rhythms inspired by new dances? Deejays Burru Banton, Flourgon and Roger Steppers attempt to get to the bottom of it:

Burru: 'It both. In Jamaica, we keep changing our style of dancing and then the rhythms will be changed a little to suit it, like if people started moving double time or something, but then when completely new rhythms appear somebody will start a dance to go with it.'

Reggie: 'They go together most of the time, or nobody can tell which came first. The Bogle dance came out just after the rhythm, Buju play the tune first, then the dance appear …'

Flourgon: '… what about the Giggy? That was a rhythm created from a dance that was created because somebody was insane – there was a madman dancing down at Crossroads and a producer went down there. Watch him dance and he built a rhythm right after and that's how the Giggy came about.'

Burru : 'If some artist see a little youth doing a dance in the dancehall and he like the dance he may copy it and sing a song about it. Another artist may then change the name of that dance to something that suit a lyric that he's already doing and it might take off that way, so one thing can become another.'

Flourgon: 'But now there's so many videos, any dance will get taken up quicker and whoever is doing that particular song will claim it, never mind if they thought it up or not, and then it will be named after that tune.'

So it's still about as clear as what came first, rock steady the dance or the style? And were people dancing the reggae before anybody made a reggae tune?

11
beyond the bassline

Shaka Demus

Reggae without a bassline?

Ask any roots purist and
they'll tell you it can't happen.
And up until the mid-1980s,
it would have seemed like
they were making sense.

Or at least to a certain degree, because for the 20 years prior to that, since rock steady replaced ska and the electric bass guitar took over from the stand-up model, the bassline had been the heartbeat of Jamaican music. The opening page of any modern Jamaican songwriter's book. That fat bassline made the sound systems so special and drove the dancers to rhapsody and back again. Mess with that and you might as well have stayed at home. Then, in late-1985, the King Jammy-produced 'Under Me Sleng Teng' didn't bother with that bottom end and swept all before it to become the dancehall sensation of the times. Within weeks, literally hundreds of 'Sleng Teng' versions were hitting the decks across Kingston and its cultural diaspora.

The tune's structure and execution were simplicity itself: it was a rock rhythm discovered by Noel Bailey on a Casio keyboard so basic it was little more than a child's toy; the beats were slowed slightly but there were few frills added other than the necessary chords; Wayne Smith's apparently

ad-libbed, entirely uncomplicated lyric praised the herb superb; and the buzzsaw-like drone of the delivery redefined 'rudimentary'. But the result was so compelling a piece of music that for several months (a lifetime in reggae's accelerated timescale) it became something of a challenge to walk around without hearing the 'Sleng Teng' rhythm in your head, a situation not helped by the fact it was blaring out of cars, shops, open windows and radios every few yards. Given this overwhelming popular endorsement, reggae without a bassline had more than a certain rationality to it.

However, to fixate on 'Sleng Teng' would be to oversimplify. True, it was a major creative watershed on the road from roots to dancehall, but as with so many other major creative watersheds in the previous three decades of Jamaican music, ditching the bassline was a far more involved process than one moment of inspiration. Such a move had been simmering for some time, there were a number of contributing factors and a sizeable cast of characters. It was also, as you might expect by now, a development that progressed along several parallel lines. In fact, it's safe to say that by the time 'Sleng Teng' dropped, these new sounds and styles were more inevitable than remarkable. And this was for more reasons than just a sound system operator wanting an edge over the competition, although it would be daft to rule that out of the equation.

Given the continuing cyclical nature of Jamaican music, it was due a radical shift – one-drop reggae had been around for a dozen or so years, and roots' international adventures had greatly prolonged that aspect's active life. By the beginning of the 1980s, there was a generation of Jamaican youth coming of age who knew little other than roots reggae and were aware that it was increasingly irrelevant to their lives. The most obvious disparity being that after a decade of piety and righteousness the only changes – economic, social and political – to have taken place had been for the worse. To a 19-year-old sound system follower, all that chanting down Babylon seemed like so much wasted breath. It looks like we're going to get shafted anyway, so why not have some fun? And as for the hereafter, what about the here and now? Hence pleasures of the flesh became the order of the day in a return to the bawdy Caribbean traditions of slackness.

Alongside such a situation, and just as important, was another of Jamaican music's recurring themes: its periodical retreating into itself. Usually this occurs once the music goes too wide, therefore ceasing to belong to the people who created it. This regular return to its grass roots – the sound system crowds – has been happening since ska, and is how successive generations maintain a nationalistic feeling of pride with something that is uniquely theirs. Both tangibly and culturally. It's important not to underestimate how vital this is to a psyche still recovering from the dispossession that was central to successful slave trading.

By this time, the extent of roots reggae's international success had meant any sense of loss was acute – in the highest profile cases, it had shifted its criteria to the degree that it could be perceived at home as just another exotic strain of pop music that was paying more attention to the western marketplace than the West Kingston sound systems. Bob Marley may have been a Jamaican popular icon, but his music had long since ceased to cut much ice at the lawn dances. For reggae's primary audience it was a satisfying act of defiance to turn to words and music that, to the new fans, would be seen as diametrically opposed to the previous almost hippieish values.

And of course there was a pragmatic side to this musical revolution. Since the late-1970s, computers had been increasingly used in the island's studios, as those working abroad brought back the equipment they'd been coming to grips with. In the years prior to 'Sleng Teng', this became a full-scale invasion as equipment costs fell and functionality and availability increased. So while creative curiosity played a big part, the next phase in Jamaican music was always going to be digital as it was sound thinking to replace costly and often argumentative session players with a rack full of technology.

Initially these ideas bubbled through in the starker, horn-free, computer-friendly backing tracks supplied by the Roots Radics band behind such established singers as Gregory Isaacs, Dennis Brown, Barrington Levy and Sugar Minott. Then, as the next decade rolled around, the style began seriously to define itself as what it remains best known for – deejays chatting outrageous sex lyrics – which is where the real musical shift took place.

Two producers did most to establish those credentials, former-Technique Winston Riley and Volcano sound system owner Henry 'Junjo' Lawes, and the deejays they brought through included General Echo – among his initial albums were *The Slackest LP* and *12" Of Pleasure* – Lone Ranger, Clint Eastwood, Ranking Toyan, Eek-A-Mouse and the incomparable Yellowman. But it was the rush of deejays in their slipstream that put the music right back in touch with the mood of the streets, in exactly the same way the likes of Big Youth and Dillinger had done more than 10 years previously. Characters like Brigadier Jerry, Ranking Joe and Fat Head may have got the record deals, but there was a whole host of others who could make themselves heard without the support system a singer needed as they'd simply take up the mic at a sound system and rock the crowd. Once again, there was virtually no difference between the artists and the audiences, and the rank and file grabbed their chance to participate with both hands. Talent flooded in and the art of deejaying became more and more, er, progressive.

Presentation and trickery took over from portentous lyrical content as the key to success, so while performers started dressing the part – gold chains were regulation, in an antithesis to roots'n'

culture – microphone styles included high-speed delivery, wild scatting, two-handed vocals and more 'oinks' and 'ribbits' than a noisy farmyard. It was these street-level, more spontaneous deejays who pushed the producers into delving deeper and deeper into their new computers to find evermore challenging backing tracks. Which in turn inspired the microphone masters to greater heights.

With considerable assistance from developing technology, dancehall evolved at a ferocious rate. Looking to deliberately distance themselves from the past and given the potentially limited number of musical options within the conventional Jamaican structures for a deejay-led style, guys as bold as Riley, Lawes or their successor King Jammy's were almost duty bound to attempt life without a bassline. If they hadn't somebody else would've.

Which only leaves one matter to be settled: can it still be reggae if it doesn't have a bassline? This really comes down to how terminology changed as Jamaican music advanced internationally. Up until the end of the 1960s, different styles had different names and 'reggae' was just one more in the succession from JA boogie, ska and rock steady, each one with fundamental structural changes more or less as radical as those in 'Sleng Teng'. So to say reggae has to have a bassline is true. Technically. But, in terms of volume and impact, Jamaican music succeeded on a worldwide basis, and reggae, a particular stylistic term, became a generic term, so there is no reason whatsoever why a new development in reggae has to have a bassline anymore than rock steady needed ska's tempo.

So the answer is yes and no.

Above: At home with 'Sleng Teng' producer, King Jammy's

Left: Shaka Demus and Pliers on the beach

Bounty Killer: Dancehall Meets Pop

Throughout the last 40 years of Jamaican music conquering the world, mainstream success and home-crowd credibility have seemed mutually exclusive. 'My Boy Lollipop' was somehow never taken as seriously as anything by The Skatalites; the late-1960s stringsed-up reggae was little more than a laughing stock in specialist circles and arguments rage on as to whether Shaggy is reggae or not. But the Bounty Killer seems to have walked that line with considerable swagger. He could never be accused of diluting his somewhat abrasive delivery yet it is becoming something of a household sound in both the UK and the USA, having added his skills to records by such pop-chart regulars as No Doubt and The Fugees. It's not really that difficult, he claims, merely a matter of keeping it real:

'I try to keep it Jamaican. Whatever I do I try to bring a little Jamaican with it, so it's unique and it's different. That's what people want when they come looking for me, so that's what I give them – some artists they go overseas and see other styles and try to copy them, but that's not what the people in that country want and it's not something you can bring back to Jamaica. I'm not going to go to America and trying to do some American dream! I'm going to America to do what I does in Jamaica, because I'm a Jamaican therefore everything I do is for me and Jamaica – I can't do anything for the world if Jamaica's not accepting it.

'They say that the tone and the accent is wrong for the rest of the world, but that's my tone and my accent is supposed to say Jamaica. Sometimes I heard these artists on record and they lose their Jamaican accent, then they lost their culture and they lost their music. Then when they come home to Jamaica they've got nothing to present in Jamaica except their nationality, and the rest of the world don't want them because they don't sound like no Jamaican – they want the dancehall flavour but they're not getting enough of it.

'The song I did with No Doubt is a dancehall song … it's just a pop group doing a dancehall song because it's a straight dancehall beat. It was produced by a dancehall producer and played by a dancehall producer featuring a dancehall artist. So it's all dancehall, the only difference is No Doubt singing. So that's where dancehall is at, Number Six in the Billboard charts. Pure dancehall and I've seen all these white people reacting to it like every other music. They never was trying to absorb it differently from no other music, so I know that my music – pure dancehall – is normal. It just need the backing like any other music.'

The Advent of 'Sleng Teng'

The digital reggae single 'Under Me Sleng Teng' changed the music for ever, as it was the first to dispense with a conventional bassline. It was made in 1985 at King Jammy's, and he remembers it well.

'Wayne Smith, one of my artists, was here with a lot of other guys and Noel Bailey, they used to jam out in the yard, rehearse. One night, in 1984, Noel came to me to tell me he was playing with this little Casio keyboard that they used to practise songs

Gussie Clarke, one of modern reggae's most influential producers

with and he'd found a rhythm come up on it that was a good rhythm, but was going much too fast. He said it was like an electric tempo, going at a hundred miles an hour. He asked me if I could find the rhythm and programme back the keyboard to slow it down, which I did. It wasn't really difficult and that's how we created "Sleng Teng" on the Casio keyboard.

'It was just the drum and the bass in that keyboard, but I got it to a tempo I liked and we said let's go in the studio straight away and record it. At that time, I only had a quarter-inch, four-track machine, so we recorded the drum and bass on one track, from the Casio machine, and we over-dubbed the piano then overdubbed the percussion instruments and that was "Sleng Teng".

'We voiced it the next day. That song was the first song voiced on that rhythm because Wayne

had it already written and had the tune, all he was waiting for was the right rhythm. Now that was found he fitted the tune to it.

'As soon as we put the rhythm on the tape we knew this was a step forward for reggae because it was so different to anything else that was around. When I started to play it for other people I knew it was a good rhythm because I was getting feedback from people, Bunny Lee and King Tubby himself, but I didn't know how much it would go and how fast it would go. When I first take it a play it on my sound system, the whole place pop up. That tune played almost the whole night, just lick it back, lick it back, lick it back! And we have different versions of it, different people singing on the rhythm, so we play all of those version plus the deejays used the rhythm to deejay. It was like a whole hour and a half of pure "Sleng Teng" time.'

Elephant Man On The Importance Of A Good Stage Show

'When I was growing up, the deejays I checked out were Shabba, Ninjaman, Tiger and Super Cat. Me like them man with vibes, where they can perform. Shabba Ranks is mad 'pon stage, Ninjaman same way. Me admire the great performer. Lieutenant Stitchie great performer too, I like those deejay that you can say, "Yeah, me can feel the energy". So I work hard on my stage show because I feel it's in my blood. I want it that people come out and enjoy their money, I don't want them to come and say "Well it could've been better" and them people come and fold their arms and look. You have to give them a show for their money and that's worth working for.

'It is actually a problem that many deejays don't put on a show, because the people done hear the forty-five already. So for me, or any deejay, to come back and come do the forty-five same way on stage is wrong – the audience just stand up and say they could just play the CD on the stereo and save their money. If you're just a deejay with a tune and you come to stand up all night then people going to yawn and wanna sleep. You have to have people sweat and laugh, keep everybody on the vibes. When they go and watch Elephant Man they will have a good night and get excited for their money.

Ce'Cile

Ladies In The Dancehall

Ce'Cile is one of dancehall's newest stars, but it wasn't her first career choice as her first loves are singing and songwriting and she would rather have been an Anita Baker-type diva.

'I used to like it [dancehall] as a spectator, back in the late-1980s, but I didn't see myself doing it... Seeing performers like Tanya Stephen and Lady Saw helped. It's always better when you see other females performing, even though Lady Saw was a bit more risqué, they were like an inspiration to me'

Lady Saw, aka Marion Hall, is the Millie Jackson of dancehall reggae. Her song titles include 'Stab Up The Meat' and, ahem, 'Peanut Punch Mek Man Shit Up Gal Bed'. She's been banned from performing in some Jamaican parishes and specialises in making male audience volunteers squirm. At one particularly memorable show, she was squatting over one hapless guy's face when her shorts tore all the way down the long seam; rather than rush for the wings she put the mic to her mouth and announced: 'You're three inches away from it, and you're just looking at it!' Yet in spite of any apparent outrage, Lady Saw and her music have featured in numerous advertising campaigns and most recently she's made inroads into the American market when she was invited to collaborate with No Doubt on their most recent album. Understandably, she has strong views about what she should and shouldn't say in her records.

'I have a lot of female fans because a lot of my songs are defending them. My songs are telling them how to use the muscle and grip on it, you know? And if men try to put them down I'll build them up. I'll never put down a woman, and my songs are not cussing them. I'm not doing anything sexual on stage – no raw sex, but I'll talk about it.

'If people say it's too vulgar, I'll just tell them to mind their own business, because slackness has been around for a long time. Yellowman and all them guys from back in the day, they used to do it. It's just that I'm a woman, so I don't get away with things. Even now on the radio in Jamaica, men will do a record with sex in it, but if I do a record with sex in it the deejay have to play it by accident and then when he realise he wheel up the thing or go to commercial.

'It's a double standards thing, guys say stuff like how they do their woman in this position and it's fine, but if try to say I like it in this position it will never get played. So I don't care about people and what they say, I always get strength. Whenever they bug me, I get more strength and go out there and do my stuff.'

12
a return to roots

Buju Banton

Jamaica's inner-city social problems seem to be escalating, as crime and violence become the norm. But as a reaction to this, and what many see as increasing negativity in the music, the last few years have brought a resurgence of righteousness.

Downtown Kingston in 2002 isn't a wonderful place to be. Conventional forces of law and order have all but departed, leaving in their place a Godfather-style hierarchy of local dons and their enforcers. Nothing moves without these unelected mayors getting involved. They make the rules, control the cash flow, mediate disputes and pass sentence with a ruthlessness that would make Tony Soprano shudder. It's these guys' self-protective approach to town planning that has subdivided areas like Jones Town, Trenchtown and Rema into rigidly sectarian garrison communities, so precisely defined that many residents haven't crossed certain roads for years. And, in the foreseeable future, aren't all that likely to. Ghetto fabulous without the fabulous.

But we're in Jamaica. If human spirit as powerful as it is on this island could be bottled, it would put the rum industry out of business in quarter of an hour. Some of the brightest signs of hope are on those same street corners where things seem at their absolute darkest: the guy

selling sugar cane from a cart with a sign reading 'Future WalMart!'; Reggae Boyz replica football shirts are worn with a swagger that could dry washing; and everywhere you can see swathes of red, green and gold – on clothing, car trim, flags, awnings, paint jobs on houses, shops, shacks and shrubbery.

These conspicuous displays of dread are far more prevalent than a) Jamaica's official national colours; and b) they were five years ago, and are the result of, once again, yout' of all ages turning to Rasta as a manifestation of rebellion as much as a spiritual gratification. This time around though, Rastafari has a very different way of doing things than it did in Bob Marley's day.

Extreme times call for extreme measures, and the most obviously hardline reaction to Jamaica's worrying cocktail of social ills and an apparent 'degeneracy' within the music is the resurgence of the Bobo Ashanti house of Rastafari. It has been dubbed 'the Taliban of Dread' by some members of

Luciano

the media, and while this is an unfortunate choice of words, I feel it's not entirely without perception. This orthodox branch of Rastafari is rigidly disciplined, with a set of practices that puts them at odds with, well, most of modern society, and a regard for Babylon that incorporates purging by fire. Best known among the Bobo are Sizzla, Anthony B and Capleton, whose rallying cries of 'More fire!' tend to make most people's idea of Rastafari – shaped by how it was packaged when Bob Marley was alive, underpinned in Morgan Heritage's 'You don't haffi dread' world view – come across as a happy-clappy, zonked-out, more or less inclusive brand of black hippiedom. Witness the Bobo deejays' lyrical attacks on Catholicism, which, worryingly, have been taken literally by their more impressionable fans, resulting in a spate of churches being firebombed in Jamaica.

Bobo Ashanti is a branch of Rastafari that dates back to the late-1950s, when Emmanuel Edwards established his Ethiopian Black Africa International Congress Rasta camp in one of Kingston's worst ghettos. A staunch Garveyite, while Edwards advocated back-to-Africa he understood this was as much a psychological as a physical situation, thus his branch of Rastafarianism adopted – and adhered to – a grab bag of ancient Ethiopian/Old Testament ideals. Within the family, men were Kings, women Empresses and children Princes and Princesses. Several families lived within one community, with the commune as a whole being as self-sufficient as possible – vegetables were grown in their camps and arts and crafts sold. The diet contained no meat, wheat or salt; fasting was frequent in the compounds, as was prayer. A greeting would be 'Bless' or 'Blessed'. Back then, the strict codes of dress immediately set the Bobo dreads apart from their less orthodox Rasta brethren – the white robes (trimmed with red, green and gold) and the almost vertical turbans frequently drew the wrath of the colonial authorities.

Today, it's these turbans – a sheet of material rolled tightly around the wearer's dreadlocks – that provide a striking illustration of why Bobo is back with this degree of strength. Post-Bob Marley, dreadlocks – the very essence of Rasta's identity in Babylon – had become a fashion statement rather than a statement of intent, so to cover them in this manner removes such confusion and presents a clear show of identity to the world. And this in itself provides a handy metaphor for most of what Bobo 2002 is about. Look beyond the blistering Papal denunciations and the notion of fire as an instrument of social change and there's little difference between Bobo's ideology and what was on offer before Rasta went so wide as to spread the righteousness unacceptably thin. Indeed, at the core of this rise of Bobo is a steady-handed refocusing of what Rasta ought to stand for coupled with a refusal to be pulled into any form of compromise.

Check it: back at the start of the 1970s, homosexuality was considered an abomination, Rasta women had to dress and behave with modesty and were kept apart from the community while on their periods. The camps both in and around Kingston functioned as self-supporting co-operatives. The Bible was studied avidly, alcohol was strictly forbidden, acts of piety were observed and ganja was smoked *au naturel* in a chalice to avoid contamination from gummed paper or tobacco. To wear dreadlocks was an act of equal parts defiance and sufferation as it brought upon the wearer the authorities' routine brutalisation and the many non-believers' contempt. Even Bobo's apparent aggressiveness has a precedent: 30 years ago, Rasta actively sought folk-devil status as a means of striking terror into the heart of Babylon – the idea of 'dread' didn't come about by chance,

Capleton

Left: Cocoa Tea, at the forefront of reggae's new roots movement: 'The music I make try to uplift the people and teach the world something.'

Right: Sizzla

and so-called respectable Jamaican parents would scare their children with bogeyman-type tales of Rastas coming to get them

Thus a great deal of the Bobo Ashanti's appeal to those seeking a path of righteousness in millennial Jamaica is that it has put the goalposts back where they used to be as regards spirituality, sense of purity and escape from what's going on around them. Songs like Anthony B's 'Fire Pon Rome' and 'Repentance Time', or Capleton's 'Pure Sodom' and 'Burn Dem Dreadie' or Sizzla's 'Attack' are exciting, hardcore blasts that tend to sweep the listener along more than fill any holes left by an apparent lack of radicalism elsewhere. But the basic problem lies with how this relates to the year 2002, hence the justification in the Taliban comparisons. The world and its approach to morality has moved on since the early 1970s – advocating a homosexual holocaust is unlikely to bring Bobo Ashanti mainstream support. Such is their contempt that one deejay's recent UK dates were billed as the 'Burn The Chi Chi Men Tour' on all promotional material. And such is the way commercialism has embraced the world, Bobo's peddling of handmade straw brooms on the street (even the stars have to take their turn as a way of staying humble) can be difficult for many to come to terms with under the McDonald's and Ralph Lauren signs that litter the Kingston landscape.

The way in which much of Jamaica is reacting to Bobo is once again a throwback to Rasta's 1970s heyday, albeit with a general level of official tolerance that is a great deal higher than before, its very nature provoking extreme reactions. Many ordinary people are concerned about the cultish aspect of the community structures, particularly in light of so much youthful disaffection in Jamaica at the moment; they fear it could present a particularly attractive alternative. Good Christians take the line that any kind of Rasta is heathen, and, understandably, take great umbrage at the 'Fire Pon Rome' line of thinking. It's this same fierceness that appeals to many youths – confrontational lyrics, hardcore rhythms, in your face deliveries – and has given Bobo records a place in the dancehall. While a large fanbase may not go so far as to wear a turban, they go along with the whiff of violence involved.

Musicians and producers with no vested interest seem to want to judge on a musical level, refusing to get drawn into theological debates. Tellingly, older dreads are split. Half are taking the line that any form of Rasta is preferable to the nihilism around them. The other side, however, proclaims the new wave of Bobo Ashanti to be false prophets, citing several prominent artists' past exploits and current followings (Sizzla and Capleton both have histories of gun and gal records and retain much of their old fanbases) as being too close to for spiritual comfort. These critics feel sure that it's only a matter of time before the turban assumes the same style-accessory status as dreadlocks did.

Not that this is of much concern to Bobo's young self-styled warrior priests (another ancient Ethiopianism). Ominously, in Jamaica in spring 2002, when asked where Bobo will go next, more than one told me: 'The time for preaching is over, now is the time for gathering.'

Luciano entertains Primrose Hill Primary School

Luciano

Luciano is one of the new wave of roots artists who seem to be harking backwards as much they are looking forwards. He draws immediate comparisons with Bob Marley for his simplistic, countrified approach to life and has a way with his songs that remind us reggae is very much a folk music. The acoustic guitar is Luciano's weapon of choice, and he has gained something of a reputation for being anti-technology, but in spite of his way of doing things he actually has no problem with computers as such in today's reggae … just with the people who are using them:

'Now with me and the computer, this renaissance in the computer is not really the problem of the computer. It's with mankind lending themselves to allow the computer to think for them. To me, the creativity of the mind must always be maintained and it's the same thing with the music. So we use technology because, once upon a time we are going into the studio and you have to see lots of wires and big tubes before you could get any sound out of it, now with modern technology and computers it's much easier in the studio.

'So give thanks for technology, and it's when we use our minds and our creativity along with the technology that we get the best results out of the studio and out of life. But it can go too far. If you forget about the natural instruments and play everything on synthesisers then you lose the feel and the vibration that come with making music. It's like with life, we have to maintain the authenticity of our lives in order to be able to make good use of the technology – you can cook with microwave, but you won't know what you are doing with it unless you've first learned to make your fire, make your pot and bake your pudding, natural. If all you know is microwave you can't progress because you don't really understand what cooking is.

'I'm not really hitting against technology, but remember His Majesty says, technology we cannot fight because the mind of man is so creative that we gonna create things that, if we not careful, create ourselves out of existence. Our inventions are things that destroy us. It's us that can be the problem.'

Buju Banton

Roots deejay Buju Banton is a direct descendant of the Maroons, runaway slaves who in the seventeenth century occupied Cockpit Country, Jamaica's interior. Under the leadership of the legendary fighter Cudjoe and a woman known as Queen Nanny, they carried out guerrilla-style raids on plantations, burning crops and stealing livestock, while offering a safe haven to other slaves. Although the British brought in dogs to track them, they kept their rebellion active for 50 years and eventually forced the colonial authorities to negotiate.

The word Maroon was given to the rebels by the Spanish as it comes from their word *cimarron* which means 'wild', which would seem somehow apt when applied to Buju Banton. Never far from controversy, he may have converted from badman-ism to Rastafari, but he remains unreservedly unrepentant as regards the 'Boom Bye Bye' affair. Here he discusses his Maroon heritage.

'I was born in Kingston, but my family, my mother's mother, is a direct descendant of the Maroons. They were the people who rebel against the British, who fought so strong and intelligent that the British couldn't quell their uprising and in the end they were given free land and the sort of rights that would be unheard of back in slavery days.

'They were also an ancient people from Africa who brought ancient traditions over and still maintain certain traditions and festivities direct from the motherland. That's why they didn't bow down, because their situation made them into what they were, because they had to fight and rebel against the oppressors and the colonial masters. It was an awful struggle.

'Although I am descended from them, I'm no more a fighter than any other black man. If any black man is in the West he is a fighter, a survivor, because they have been surviving years of hardship which they have not created on themselves. Every black man have to fight because if him don't fight then him ultimately becomes null and void. For survive you have to fight – in this day, for I not to fight this day would be meaningless. When we say fight, we mean going out there and meeting people, where you have to stand up for what is right, for our right. That is the fight today, and it is the same fight as the Maroons had hundreds of years ago.'

Anthony B in Ladbroke Grove

'More Fire'

'More Fire' is a Bobo catch phrase and is open to misinterpretation with sometimes fatal results. Anthony B explains what it is meant to mean:

'A lot of people misunderstood what we are doing. A lot of kids out there take a lot of things that we say to extremes. But we are not the ones to be blamed for it, because learning things when you are young, it takes time to grow to maturity for you to really gain understanding. So when sometimes we say burn the fire, somebody else would take the fire and go and burn somebody. We didn't say to that person go and burn that person, but they take it to extremes.

'When we say burn the fire we are not saying, take a match and go light somebody. Literally, what we are saying is get rid of these things that is no good to humanity, burn these things out of your system. Just like you got some garbage in your house, you get rid of it, put it in the fire.

'I burn fire for Butch Stewart, the general manager of Air Jamaica, also the owner of Sandals hotel in Jamaica, and we see a lot of the oppression of the system of Jamaica is caused by these people. We say burn fire for PJ Patterson, the Prime Minister. We burn the opposition leader who is Edward Seaga ... we burn the minister of security. When we say these things, it's not from a racial point of view, nor from a crazy point of view, nor from a fanatical point of view. We're saying these things from the experience point of view, where these people is the oppressor of our country. "Fire Pon Rome" means get rid of the oppressors.'

where next?

2002, and the story of Jamaican music has made itself heard across the world to such a degree and with such apparent ease, you wonder why other musics haven't done so. Or, at least, you'll wonder that for about three or four minutes before you realise that not much else has got reggae's spirit. But the truly pleasing thing about this state of affairs is the apparent strength reggae enjoys as an international cultural force. And it has established itself as such on its own terms too: rather than founder in Bob Marley's slipstream – as many were certain it would – reggae renewed itself to gatecrash the worlds of rap, rock and R&B with a conviction that even the most festival-friendly roots acts never quite managed.

It seems as if reggae has finally worked out how to satisfy the parochial and the international markets at the same time, and sell itself in all its pomp rather than offer up what big record companies assume the general public can stand. The fact that the uncompromising Bounty Killer and Lady Saw were invited to contribute to No Doubt's last album illustrates this point perfectly, as they're not there to show off their table manners and they don't. If Gwen and co. had wanted cute they would've sent for Shaggy. And as dancehall gains its footholds in MTV, Busta Rhymes isn't above putting his Jamaican roots to work and so furthering the cause. In the UK too, on the current garage scene So Solid Crew talk about their reggae roots with such enthusiasm you know that if it

wasn't for the sound system scene shaping their approach to what they do, they'd probably be a male-voice choir. Or not, but you get the idea.

Back in Jamaica, the prospects offered up by this international activity haven't been ignored. One of the brightest hopes for the future is T.O.K., a group of four formally-trained singers, who cite Boyz II Men as their role-model act, are as at home with Platters-style doo wop or contemporary R&B balladeering as they are with dancehall deejaying and the rawest ragga lyrics. While so much of their output is aimed squarely at the USA, where they deservingly have a record deal, they haven't forgotten where it all comes from. Witness their 'Chi Chi Man' song: all manner of tricky vocal arrangements and quasi-classical instrumentation make it as intriguing and engaging a four minutes as you'll hear anywhere, yet the subject matter speaks so exclusively to the quartet's 'home crowd' that the audience outside of Jamaica's dancehalls are roundly offended. Once they work out what it's about, that is. Likewise Ce'Cile, who fully understands the role of the female deejay in the twenty-first century, plays the sex card in trumps and has broadened out her act to include as much singing as deejaying. They are the latest in this new wave of Jamaican invaders that demonstrate how far reggae has continued beyond the stewardship of Bob Marley's extraordinary career.

But where next? Reggae 'pon the moon? Maybe that's not such a ridiculous idea.

Picture Credits

Dennis Morris 5; 6; 8; 11; 14; 19; 21; 32; 36; 41 (t); 42; 44; 45; 46; 51; 52; 55; 56; 57; 58; 62; 64; 65; 67; 69; 72; 74; 80; 81; 82; 83; 85; 86; 87; 88; 93; 95; 97; 98; 101; 104 (t, bl); 105; 106; 107; 110; 111; 112; 113; 115; 116–17; 120; 123; 126 (t); 128; 130; 131; 134 (b); 137; 138; 139; 140; 141; 142; 144; 146; 147; 149; 150; 152; 156–57

Topham 10; 24; 25; 48

Urbanimage.tv 13; Tim Barrow 29; 37; 96; 99; 119; 134 (t); 145; Wayne Tippetts 93; 124; Jean Bernard Sohiez 135

The *Jamaican Gleaner* 23

David Corio 30; 39; 63; 70; 89; 121; 124 (b); 143; 147; 151

Chris Morrow 18; 29; 41 (br, bl); 47; 49; 104 (br)

Pictorial Press 16; 35; 90; 154

Redferns Ebert Roberts 27; Andrew Putler 40; Michael Ochs Archives 73

***Ragga* Magazine** 31

London Features International 50

The Kobal Collection 66

Rex Features 78

Bunny Lee 54

Every effort has been made to contact all copyright holders. The publishers would be pleased to hear if any oversights or omissions have occurred.

Index

Page references in bold indicate major sections, and those in italics indicate illustrations.